The Road to Elmira

Volume 1

The Road to Elmira

Volume 1

Rich Kendall

Rich Kendall Books

All quotes by Seth or Jane Roberts used by permission of Rick Stack and New Awareness Network, Inc.

Editorial by Sue Williams

This book is set in 11½-point Arno Pro
Design and composition by Brad Walrod/Kenoza Type

Library of Congress Control Number: 2011906236

Library of Congress subject headings
New Age movement
Altered states of consciousness
Lightning Source (Firm)

ISBN 978-0-9835776-0-7

First Edition

Printed in the United States of America

1 3 5 7 9 10 8 6 4 2

Visit www.richkendallbooks.com

Dedicated to Jane Roberts
(May 8, 1929–September 5, 1984)

Prologue

The official story of our lives takes place within one time period, upon one planet, and within a given number of years. Yet there are other stories waiting to be told, as lanterns lit in taverns centuries ago continue burning.

Perhaps one day I'll get to tell some of those other stories, but for now, this one will have to do.

Rich Kendall
June 7, 2011

1

All Roads Do Not Lead to Rome

I was nineteen years old in 1969, and changes in the mass consciousness of this country had been bubbling up for some time, and in some cases the bubble just burst.

In November of 1969 approximately 250,000 people marched on Washington, D.C. to protest our involvement in the Vietnam War, a war that had divided the country into warring factions of its own.

That same year, close to 500,000 people converged on a dairy farm in upstate New York to attend a music festival which came to be known as Woodstock. I was one of those people, and while there was definitely plenty of music, I'll never forget the scores of people lying by the side of the road, waylaid by bad drug trips, clothes soaked and muddy from all the rain, and underneath it all an unspoken awareness that the Hippie revolution that had sought to make the world over into a Mecca of peace and love was coming to an end.

The movie *Easy Rider* made its way to the wide screen that year as Peter Fonda and Dennis Hopper traveled by motorcycle in a horizontal direction in search of the real America. Neil Armstrong took a vertical route and became the first man to walk on the moon.

By the end of the decade the ideology of the 1960s had reached its crescendo, and within a few years yesterday's hippies would become today's lawyers, doctors, and Wall Street brokers. For some, this transition was relatively easy. For me, thoughts of finding a steady job; settling down; focusing on making money—all these goals were anathema to the hippie spirit that still lived within me.

As I held on tight to my counterculture stance I knew I risked being left behind. But how to find a place for myself in a world I had railed against was a dilemma I did not know how to solve. So as the decade drew to a close, uncertainties hung in the air all around me.

There was only one thing I felt for certain: I needed some answers before I could move on with my life, answers to a few simple, basic questions. Questions such as Why am I here? Is there a God? What happens to us when we die? Have I lived before? Why is there so much suffering in the world? As I said, just a few simple, basic questions.

I proceeded to search for the answers in various ways. One of the avenues I tried was drugs, but the "insights" I received during those seemingly heightened states of awareness had a nasty way of turning into so much pulp as the drug's effects would begin to wear off.

For many people, traditional religion seemed to work. After all, "In God We Trust" is not only written on much of our currency but is actually our national motto. But I could not place my trust in a god who without hesitation would destroy the entire earth, me included, if I did not follow his rules and worship him on a regular basis.

As I continued my search I kept running into one dead end road after another. I'm reminded of a movie I saw as a young teenager called *A Hatful of Rain*. There is this one scene in the movie where a young boy named Johnny is told that if he works very hard, money will magically appear in his pocket. So with great enthusiasm Johnny goes out into the field and starts digging and digging. He keeps checking his pockets but to his dismay no money appears. Undeterred, Johnny continues to dig. It's a warm day and as Johnny begins to perspire he takes off his hat and puts it down beside him. It then starts to rain and the hat starts filling up with water, but Johnny is too busy digging to notice. With his pockets still empty, a disappointed Johnny decides to go home. He puts his hat back on his head and as he does so all the water that had collected inside of it pours all over him.

All Johnny had to show for all his hard work was *A Hatful of Rain*. And that's exactly how I was starting to feel. Despite all my efforts at finding answers my pockets were empty and I felt as if I was running out of options. And then a ray of hope poked its head out from behind the horizon. A friend of mine who was also interested in spiritual matters told me about these metaphysical classes he started attending in response to an ad he saw in the newspaper. These classes were taught by a fellow named Marcel, who claimed to be a master of occult knowledge.

If you studied Marcel's teachings and followed his directions exactly as given, you would be led (according to Marcel) to various levels of enlightenment, although it was understood that you would never reach the level of enlightenment Marcel had attained.

Had I taken more time to evaluate the ideas Marcel was presenting, as well as the man himself, I might not have joined his group of faithful followers so readily. But when you're stranded on an island and a ship approaches, you don't start examining what flag it's flying; you just get on board. So with hope tucked under my sleeve, off I went to meet Marcel.

Marcel was a good looking man of African-American descent: tall, charismatic, and on the surface at least, very self-assured. It was hard to imagine Marcel being flustered by anything. He had no hesitation in letting you know that he had mastered many levels of reality and was in possession of secret and hidden knowledge to which few were privy. This knowledge, he emphasized, should not be shared with others until they were properly prepared to receive it; otherwise, doing so could be very dangerous.

Marcel attracted mostly young people, and in hindsight I can honestly say that Marcel *was* a master: a master at exploiting other people's insecurities and fears. Feelings of hopelessness combined with little faith in one's own worth provided a perfect recipe for Marcel, and he knew exactly how to mix the ingredients.

Marcel's intentions were to open a school, create an elite army of metaphysical mentors, and then set them loose upon the world to educate the "ignorant masses" and save their miserable souls. But not all the students who were studying under Marcel would be chosen to become part of this exclusive army. One day I heard through the grapevine that I was not going to be one of those selected. While I didn't know this for a fact, the possibility of being excluded did not make me very happy.

When I was in the sixth grade an announcement was made that classes were going to be divided in a new way. Special classes were being created called "SP" for those whose intelligence ranked above the norm. No tests were given and no specific criterion was offered to explain how the school would come up with a decision as to who qualified for SP and who didn't. Parents would simply receive a letter from the school board stating whether or not their son or daughter had been accepted to enter the SP program. Everyone was on the edge of their seats waiting for that letter.

I remember how terrible I felt when my parents informed me that they had received such a letter and that I was not going to be one of those invited to take part in SP. And I didn't feel much better when two weeks later my parents received another letter from the school stating that they had decided to accept me after all. I knew there was more to this than met the eye, and I figured there was probably some problem in filling up some of the classes—hence my newly-found intelligence miraculously rising to the surface.

Trying out for a school team or school play and not making the cut or not being allowed to join some special group can be a difficult pill to swallow. But being denied a place in Marcel's school might also mean being denied access to that secret knowledge he so often spoke of, and the thought of that was too much for me to bear.

So I gathered up all my courage and decided to call Marcel to find out if this rumor was true. Marcel's voice on the other end of the line sounded as if it was right inside my head. He proceeded to tell me in an imperious manner that I could not be admitted to his school for the following reason: **I was in the grips of a demoniacal thing.** Let me tell you, this felt a lot worse than not qualifying for SP classes.

His words reflected my worst fears about myself—perhaps there really was something fundamentally wrong with me, and somehow I wasn't put together quite right. Maybe when I was being assembled one of the mechanics picked up the wrong screw or the wrong bolt, and by the time their mistake was discovered I was all sealed up and it was simply too late to do anything about it.

Looking back upon Marcel's pronouncement all those years ago I feel bad for that nineteen-year old self of mine who so willingly accepted such a proclamation without question. But if one were to start questioning any of the actions Marcel took or the statements he made, one ran the risk that the entire house of cards would collapse, a risk I just wasn't willing to take.

Marcel however did throw me a bone. He told me that although I couldn't be part of his school, I could continue studying his philosophy from the outside, and if I read certain books in the order he told me to read them, I could find some measure of enlightenment. Some measure of enlightenment sounded a lot better than continuing to wander in the dark, so I was determined to follow the path he set out before me. Then, in the latter part of 1970, the winds began to shift.

2

A Door Opens

One of the students who was studying under Marcel came across a book called *The Seth Material,* by Jane Roberts. Although this book was not one of those on Marcel's required reading list, she started telling fellow students about it.

If history teaches us anything, it teaches us that word of mouth is one of the most powerful forces on earth, so word about this book spread quickly. In short time Marcel was dutifully asked if we could add this title to his reading list. He agreed to this request but conveniently left out the fact that he had already contacted Jane Roberts by phone numerous times, had asked to visit with her, and Jane was having no part of it. (All of this I was to find out about much later.) Jane did not see Marcel as a kindred spirit but as a self-deluded individual. His brand of esoteric knowledge was saturated with concepts and caveats that were completely opposite to the ideas Jane was presenting.

So while allowing us to read Jane's book, Marcel went out of his way to let us know that Jane was not very evolved spiritually and was not to be taken seriously. He did, however, decree that Seth's presence made the book worth reading, claiming that Seth was more in line with the level of metaphysical expertise that Marcel had achieved.

I can't tell you the exact date in 1970 when I first picked up *The Seth Material,* but after reading just a few pages I could feel something happening. It was as if a part of me that had been sleeping for centuries was starting to wake up. Although I was still under Marcel's spell, I wanted to go to one of those classes Jane wrote about.

In the summer of 1971 I decided to write Jane a letter asking if it would be possible to attend one of her classes. Jane wrote back saying that if I was going to be in the area during one of the nights she held class, I could stop by. She only asked that I let her know beforehand. Sounded like a fair deal to me. I proceeded to tell Marcel about the letter I had sent to Jane as well as her response, and I asked him if going to one of Jane's classes would be alright with him, and he said yes.

Summer and fall passed quickly that year, and by the beginning of December bitter winds once again held New York City in their grip. When temperatures really began to plummet, people bundled up in such a way that the only visible part of their body was their eyes, providing the only clear evidence that the creature walking toward you was of the human kind.

On one of those winter evenings I was sitting at my kitchen table enjoying a hot bowl of pea soup when the phone rang. The news that reached my ears stunned me, and for a few moments I could feel my consciousness wobble. The caller informed me that earlier in the day Marcel had dropped dead on the street. They had no further information at this point.

This just didn't seem possible. Marcel was only in his forties, extremely energetic, filled with life. How could this be? But it was.

Marcel had dropped dead on one of those cold and snowy New York City streets and no one knew for sure what the cause was. Like so many things in life this was one more mystery with no definitive answer.

As often happens when any kind of leader dies, others rush in to try to fill the void. Occasionally the right kind of person is able to keep things going, but this would not be one of those occasions.

With Marcel gone, things quickly fell apart. His fledgling army of enlightened soldiers soon went their separate ways, melting into the anonymous masses whose ignorant souls they were one day going to save.

As for me, I didn't like the idea at all that my spiritual quest was coming to an end so abruptly. I thought of writing Jane another letter, but my friend Jeff, who had also been a devotee of Marcel, offered to contact Jane directly. Thanks to Jeff's efforts, Jane agreed to let us attend one of her classes during the first week of January, 1972.

Life has a funny way of opening doors when we least expect it, and while there was certainly nothing funny about the death of Marcel, doors were being opened. There was just one pressing question that had to be answered sooner rather than later: where the heck was Elmira, New York, anyway?

3

Elmira Bound

The town of Elmira is located in the Southern Tier of central New York state. It is built almost entirely in the flood plain of the Chemung River which flows eastward through the city. A Civil War prison camp called "Hellmira" is part of the city's history, where approximately 12,000 Confederate soldiers were confined, with almost 3,000 of them dying there due to disease and poor sanitary conditions.

On the brighter side, Elmira served as home to Mark Twain, the American author and humorist. In the 1870s, overlooking the valley in Elmira, Twain penned some of his most famous works, including *The Adventures of Tom Sawyer* and *Adventures of Huckleberry Finn*.

And one final note: according to official statistics, the last Labrador Duck was seen in Elmira on December 12, 1878. How one verifies such a fact I don't know. Perhaps the very next day, shortly after this statistic was recorded, some local farmer doing his early morning chores sighted yet another Labrador Duck, and then again, for all we know, it may have been the same Labrador Duck sighted the day before. But the record has been written and I highly doubt it will ever be changed.

I'd also like to say to any historians who specialize in duck sightings that if I have offended you in any way or said anything politically incorrect, please forgive me. I have nothing against ducks, Labrador or otherwise, and to be honest, I'm not sure I'd recognize a Labrador Duck if it landed in my soup.

In any event, ducks were not the major focus of my attention this morning. Today was the day I would be going to my first (and for all I knew, my last) class taught by Jane Roberts.

The distance from New York City to Elmira was roughly two hundred forty miles. About an hour outside of the city we would pick up Route 17 which would take us the rest of the way. How ironic it seemed to me that Route 17 was going to be the main highway we would be traveling on, for along that route I'd be passing towns that evoked some of the happiest memories of my life. One of those towns was Wurtsboro, New York, home of Camp Lakota, the sleepaway camp I attended when I was about twelve years old. My first summer there was like discovering a whole new world. My counselor's grandmother owned the camp, which gave me an edge from the start. With our days built around athletic activity, and having excelled at sports, my popularity was assured. But most importantly, my counselor informally adopted me, took me under his wing so to speak. His kindness and caring is something I'll always remember.

Also along Route 17 about fifteen miles from Wurtsboro is the town of Monticello, with the Catskill Mountains rising in the background. Monticello was where my family used to vacation when I was very young, and this also held fond memories for me.

Passing by Wurtsboro and Monticello for the first time in many years reminded me of those relatively carefree days. Part of me longed to return to those times, but time doesn't honor such wishes. Today was January 4, 1972, and I had a date with the universe. One might have even called it a "blind date," for I truly had no idea what to expect.

4

Judge Not That You Be Not Judged

Jane Roberts and her husband Robert F. Butts lived in an old Victorian on West Water Street, with the Chemung River chugging quietly along just a short distance away. They rented two apartments on the second floor, and as I climbed the flight of stairs that led to Jane's living room, Jane happened to be standing in the hallway.

She asked me my name and when I told her it was Richard she paused for a moment, as if something had just clicked inside her head, and then asked me if I was called something else. I defensively said I was not, although in truth almost everyone still called me by my nickname, which was Dickie. I should have realized right then and there that I was in for a lot more than I had bargained for.

As I entered the room where class would be taking place, the first thing that struck me was the people who had gathered there. Among those in attendance were schoolteachers, nurses, a fourth generation Elmiran who ran a shopping mall, a former nun, a number of local housewives—all in all not quite what I had expected.

This group of guys from New York, with our hair down to our shoulders and our rambunctious and often rebellious behavior, presented quite a contrast to those seated in Jane's living room that evening.

These folks just didn't seem to be the type who would question the nature of existence, or anything else for that matter. Yet outer appearances can often be quite deceptive.

One woman, whom I more easily envisioned leading a local PTA meeting rather than attending one of these classes, came up to me and told me she was "picking up" information about a former life of mine. She said I had been a high-class prostitute and spy during the American Revolution and that my name had been Suzanne or Suzette. According to what she "was getting," my lover at that time was a current friend of mine whose name back then had been Grimidly.

She then informed me that this Grimidly character was a military officer to whom I used to funnel secret information. She continued to provide me with various details and told me that at some point Grimidly thought I had betrayed his confidence, although in actuality I hadn't. But thinking this to be the case, he shot me in the back of the neck. She then said she was having images of me and some of my cronies as Greeks or Romans, dressed in togas with wreaths around our heads.

Not quite sure how to respond to all this information I just thanked her and then parked myself in the back of the room near the large bay windows. A few minutes later in walked Jane and placed herself in the handsome Kennedy rocking chair I had seen pictures of in *The Seth Material,* one of the first books Jane had published.

Casually dressed with jeans and a loose fitting long-sleeved top, Jane lit up a cigarette and poured herself a glass of wine. She then started talking about some recent developments involving something called Sumari. Sumari was described as a psychic family or guild of consciousness whose members worked together through the centuries to help mankind. There was also a Sumari "language," although not a language in the usual sense since it had never been verbally spoken by any group of people in our history. Despite the nature of this "non-language," Jane had recently begun singing as well as conversing in Sumari.

As class continued to speculate about the meaning of Sumari, Jane suddenly took off her glasses, placed them on the nearby coffee table, and began speaking in a loud, deep masculine voice. Along with the voice change, her facial muscles also changed. But the most striking difference had to do with her eyes.

Within every person's eyes there is an intangible quality reflecting a uniqueness that distinguishes them from all others, and at that moment, the personality that was currently looking out through Jane's eyes was clearly not Jane.

This other personality, who was known as Seth, was speaking now about the Sumari and how they were gathering together from near and far. Years later a movie called *Close Encounters of the Third Kind* came out where people also gathered together from near and far to witness an alien landing at Devils Tower, a rock formation in northeastern Wyoming. But there was nothing alien about Seth's appearance or disconcerting in any way as I watched him speak through Jane.

Then, as quickly and easily as Jane had gone into trance, she now came out of trance, She put her glasses back on, took a sip of wine, and asked class what Seth had said. After class members gave Jane a brief description of Seth's comments, she went back into trance, but instead of Seth coming through, Jane started singing. The words Jane sang did not correspond to any language I was familiar with, so I assumed this must be the Sumari language that the class had just been discussing. And although I say *Jane* was singing, the personality that was now looking out through Jane's eyes and doing the singing was neither Jane nor Seth.

Whatever this new personality was (or wasn't), the vocal gymnastics that were operating were quite impressive, as low notes and high notes were being executed with perfect pitch. As the song continued I could feel the sounds bouncing off the walls, and at times it felt like the walls themselves were doing the singing. When the song ended, various class members described their reactions and then Jane called for a break. She got up from her rocker, walked across the hall to her other apartment, and it was understood that for the next 15 minutes or so Jane was not to be disturbed.

During break, class members spoke in animated fashion about all kinds of things—dreams, coincidences, out-of-body experiences, topics that today would fall under the category of "new age." When Jane reentered the room the atmosphere was still buzzing with lots of discussions, laughter, and a feeling of camaraderie, although some of us were only meeting each other for the first time . . . or were we?

Ray was a pleasant looking young man who appeared both friendly and intelligent as he participated in class that evening. Seemingly out of nowhere, one of the class members asked the following question, directing it to no one in particular: "Why is Ray on trial?" This question was then repeated; however, this time the "no one in particular" part changed to someone very in particular: me! I was then asked why I was feeling all this anger toward Ray.

I began to squirm both within and without. My instinctive reaction was total denial, although in fact, each time Ray spoke I could feel my hostility toward him rise. In the next moment Jane went back into trance and started singing in that Sumari "language" again. While still in trance she motioned for Ray and me to walk over to her and stand on either side of her rocker. She took Ray's hands and my hands and clasped them together. As the Sumari song continued I could feel my anger toward Ray beginning to fade. I then smiled at him as if to say, "Okay, all my anger for you is now gone." Secretly however (or so I thought), I was still holding on to some of that anger. Jane then *vigorously* shook Ray's hands and my hands which were still intertwined, and with that gesture all of my anger toward Ray truly did dissipate. Ray and I laughed, released our hands, and Jane ended the song.

Before we barely had time to blink, Seth came through, looked at me, and emphatically stated, *Let that be a lesson to you!* He did not say this in a mean-spirited manner (no pun intended), and I didn't feel put down or demeaned in any way. I walked back to my seat by the bay windows, not really sure what had just transpired.

A few of the class members then said that as they were listening to the Sumari song, they had images of a trial, with me being the judge and Ray being accused of some form of sexually immoral act.

Jane said she was receiving similar images. As this judge, it seems I cut Ray no slack for his misdeeds and meted out a very severe sentence, which in effect relegated him to the role of outcast in society's eyes. I later learned that one of the purposes of the Sumari songs was to conjure up memories of events from past lives.

Jane was also picking up, as were others in the room, that Paul, a friend of Ray's, and Jeff, a friend of mine, both of whom were in class this night, were witnesses at this trial. And Bea, one of the local Elmirans who regularly attended class and who was also there this evening, was supposed to have been the scribe. At this point I was now able to admit that I had indeed been feeling anger toward Ray ever since class began, and I conceded that I was just being defensive about it when called on it. Jane simply said that we all try to deny what we are feeling at times and it was no big deal. Class ended about 11:00 that evening, and I was more awake than I had been when the day had started.

As we were driving back to New York City, Jeff mentioned how amazed he was when I started singing along with the Sumari while standing in front of Jane. Singing along with the Sumari? I honestly had no recollection of this at all, but at that point if Jeff had told me that the couch had levitated and circled the room I don't think I would have doubted it.

Few cars traveled along Route 17 this time of night, but there were plenty of trucks more than willing to keep us company. As we passed by Wurtsboro, New York I thought of my twelve-year old self at summer camp, contentedly sleeping after a long day of sports and getting into whatever kinds of mischief twelve-year old boys get into. I wondered how he might have reacted if I told him about the journey he was going to take one day. Perhaps on some level he was already aware of this, but for now he needed to be a twelve-year old boy and needed his sleep. I also needed to sleep but when I finally got home and put my head on the pillow, my mind kept tossing and turning with images from Jane's class. The whole feeling of that class was very different from what I had experienced while studying under Marcel, but having devoted the last two years of my life to Marcel's teachings, I wasn't about to abandon that path as a result of one evening in Elmira, regardless of how fascinating it was. Yet I was intent on attending another one of Jane's classes. But Jane, it seems, had intentions of her own.

5

My Own Voice

In February Jane and Rob were preparing to go on vacation, with classes scheduled to resume the first week of March. Before they left Jeff called Jane to ask if we could attend another class. Neither I nor Jeff anticipated anything other than a positive response, yet contrary to our expectations, Jane was extremely resistant to the idea of us coming back to class. She tried to discourage Jeff with comments about how crowded class was going to be and how far away we lived. To Jeff's credit he was able to impress upon Jane how much it meant to us to be able to attend another class, and Jane finally relented. I never did find out what was behind Jane's resistance, but when March rolled around we once more headed toward the town of Elmira.

It felt good to be on the road again, away from the blaring horns of the taxis and the constant grumbling of the city buses as they methodically made their way down the same streets day after day with little change in their routine—not unlike the lives of many of the passengers they carried.

As the city receded further and further, I started to wonder what the universe had in store for us tonight. As we passed by mountain streams and lush forests, it struck me that despite all of man's meddling, for the most part nature was still alive and well. Around that thought I could feel connections forming regarding my own nature, but I wasn't quite able to follow the thread or translate into words what I was feeling.

The closer I got to Elmira the more my adrenaline began to flow. With Marcel, there was always a rigid set of guidelines one was expected to follow without question and without deviation. In Jane's class, while there were basic assumptions to which we all subscribed, within those assumptions there was unlimited room for exploration.

As I entered Jane's living room for what was only the second time, I felt far more comfortable than the first visit. There were no seats available so I happily parked myself on the floor just a few feet from the rocking chair Jane was about to sit in. The phrase "at the feet of the master" came to mind, but I knew it didn't fit here. No one was presenting themselves as master (including Seth) and no one was playing the role of disciple. We were repeatedly told that each of us had access to the same knowledge and abilities to which Jane had access.

Seth came through numerous times during the evening, but the following comment of his evoked a strong reaction within me:

> Now, I am pleased that you sit and wait for me with such great attention. I would be much more pleased, however, if you waited for yourselves with as great attention, and if you listened to your own voices with as much attention as you pay to mine.

Listen to my own voice?—the voice of someone "in the grips of a demoniacal thing?" If there was a voice within me worth listening to I wondered where it had been hiding. "Come out, come out wherever you are," I thought to myself.

I also thought about the whole idea of "hearing voices" and how according to conventional thinking such occurrences were indications, at the least, of some form of mental instability. Yet Jane often heard voices and her personality structure seemed quite intact.

You must listen to the voice of the inner self and learn to work with it,
Seth told us. As I pondered that statement I realized Seth was not
referring to the voice of our ego, which frequently felt alienated from
the outside world, its decision making often being driven by fear
and distrust, but was referring to a voice that represented a part of
ourselves which Seth had called "the inner self." Unlike the ego, that
part of us did not view the outside world as a threat for it recognized
the part it played in the creation of that world, and in such recogni-
tion it naturally felt its connection with that which it had created.

Another difference between the ego and the inner self was that
the ego tended to view the personality as subject to a certain "chain
of command." Concerned that its authority could be usurped at any
time, the ego often felt the need to assert itself, even if doing so led
to cutting itself off from other aspects of the personality that were
trying to assist it. The following dream, which I shared in class one
evening, illustrates this point.

In my dream a voice began to speak through me. With great
effort I kept trying to close my mouth to prevent the voice from
coming through. The voice however, also with great effort, kept trying to keep my mouth open so it would be able to speak. The out-
come of this tug of war was that the words that finally did emerge
were so garbled as to be completely unintelligible. It was like someone trying to talk with their mouth filled with marbles. Seth then
commented on the dream:

> *You were involved in an experience in which you were trying to give*
> *voice, if you will forgive me, to those "higher" portions of yourselves*
> *that usually you still and quiet and hush without thinking. You*
> *were saying, My ego is my ego and it is me and I will not listen to*
> *any other portion of my personality who has the audacity to think*
> *it knows more than I do.*

So, contrary to what often seemed to be the case, my inner self
was trying to get through to me. Yet a frightened and stubborn ego
was often cutting the conversation short or, worse yet, hitting the
mute button so as not to allow any conversation at all.

An important point that needs to be addressed here has to do with the way we view the ego. It is fashionable in new age circles to bash the ego, and I realize I seem to be doing that here as well, so let me clarify my beliefs along these lines.

I don't believe consciousness can be neatly divided into separate pieces as one might slice up a pie, calling one portion the ego, another portion the inner self, another the entity, etc. While such labels serve as handy reference points, beneath their convenience I don't think any aspects of the psyche can literally be separated out. Seth used to say, *There are no divisions to the self,* so it follows that the so-called ego is not something that can exist apart from the rest of the self and held in one's hand as one might hold an apple or an orange.

However one might define the ego, it is a natural part of our being and as such should not be thought of as some kind of extra appendage we should strive to discard. Would you think it wise to cut off one of your toes because it was not as flexible as your fingers, or look with disdain upon your foot because it cannot accomplish the same things that can be accomplished using your hands? Your body functions best when all parts are used to their fullest capacity, and I believe the same holds true with the mind. So while recognizing some of the ego's paranoid tendencies, I think we should deal with that aspect of our consciousness as a parent might deal with a frightened child—i.e., in a loving manner. In treating the ego in such a way, we can help the ego to relax some of its more rigid tendencies and to feel more secure regarding its place in the overall structure of the personality.

As I journeyed back to New York City that night and watched the moon dip in and out of the clouds I began to sense this constant dance that occurred between inner and outer reality. But at the moment I needed a break from all the mental activity that had been stirring within me of late. The break was to be brief for, like the moon, one can hide behind the clouds only so long.

The Paper Trail

The road to Elmira was not going to be an easy one today. A major snowstorm had started to engulf most of the Northeast, and as road conditions continued to deteriorate I reminded myself that in the pursuit of truth others had faced obstacles far more daunting than snowstorms. That thought, however, provided little comfort when the car seemed dangerously close at times to spinning out of control as the tires struggled to make contact with the ground. This outer picture was a perfect reflection of my inner state, for I too often felt like I was moving on slippery ground and that it wouldn't take all that much for me to spin completely out of control.

Although arriving late and feeling a bit shaken, when we entered Jane's living room (the "we" being Jeff Marcus, Rick Stack, and myself) looks of amazement greeted us. Many of the local Elmirans who would have otherwise been at class that evening had stayed at home due to the harsh weather conditions. Yet here we were with our smiling faces after having traveled for over five hours in the middle of a very nasty snowstorm. From that night forward, Jane never again put up any resistance to our coming to class.

After we settled in, Jane began telling us about an altered state of consciousness she had recently experienced. While looking out her window she had glanced down at the street and noticed a crumpled piece of newspaper being battered about by the wind. As the wind tossed the paper to and fro, Jane started experiencing feelings of ecstasy with each takeoff and landing. While she was having this experience, Rob recorded it using an old reel-to-reel tape recorder they owned. Jane now played back portions of what Rob had recorded. The recording consisted mainly of a continuing series of oohs and ahs emanating from Jane in response to the movements of this piece of paper. The experience lasted for over an hour and although it sounded interesting I began to feel restless. I hadn't traveled two hundred forty miles in the middle of a snowstorm to listen to someone moaning in response to a crumpled up piece of old newspaper. In short, where was Seth?

As the evening progressed we moved on from the paper experience to other topics, but the later it got the more evident it became that Seth was not going to be part of the mix tonight. All that distance traveled and what would there be to show for it? What did a piece of paper being battered about by the wind have to do with helping me find a way out of the inner turmoil that was percolating just beneath the surface of my days? A part of me was living in constant fear. If one were able at that time to pull back the curtain and peek inside my interior landscape, you would have seen me running from this horrible creature that was endlessly stalking me, patiently waiting for a time when I would let my guard down just enough so it could overtake me, and that would be the end of me. Seth it seems had no problem in pulling back that curtain, since he told me in class one night that I had made my consciousness into a monster, which then seemed to pursue me. He also spoke of the innocence of consciousness and how it was beginning to return to me, but at the time I felt under attack by forces that I did not know how to contend with.

Lengthy treatises have been written about the strategies of war, exploring various military maneuvers such as frontal attacks, flank attacks, surprise attacks, and the list goes on. But how does one mount an effective counteroffensive when the attack originates from within? Where is the definitive treatise on what stratagems to adopt

the enemy within

when caught in a crossfire taking place within one's own consciousness? I felt vulnerable on all fronts as foreign invaders seemed to
be trying to dislodge me from the native soil of my psyche. I often
suffered from battle fatigue although the wars I fought were without
weapons and the face of the enemy was my own. The desire to run
for cover arose frequently, but where or how do you hide from the
contents of your own mind?

As class was starting to wind down I began thinking about that
piece of paper Jane referred to when recounting her altered state
of consciousness experience. Maybe there was something to learn
from that crumpled up piece of paper. It occurred to me that rather
than fighting the natural forces acting upon it or trying to control
them, the paper surrendered to each gust of wind blowing it about,
trusting that the universe would catch it wherever it landed. Feeling
its universe to be safe, it felt a sense of exhilaration with each gust,
an exhilaration that Jane was able to tune into.

People often speak of "the path of least resistance," but in the
case of that piece of paper, it wasn't a matter of "least" resistance,
but of no resistance. Perhaps that was the path I needed to follow,
the path that would lead me back to that innocence of consciousness
Seth had spoken of. Instead of doing battle with the forces swirling
inside of me, perhaps what I needed to do was to let those forces
carry me along, trusting as that piece of paper did that wherever I
landed I too would be safe.

As class ended I stood for a few moments in the cold night air
in front of Jane's house. Patches of ice had formed on the sidewalk,
and in the distance I could see layers of snow still covering the
highway. The fear of careening off the road became an unwelcome
but constant companion during the ride back. While I did arrive
home safely, at this point in my journey I could not share the paper's
unwavering belief in a cosmic safety net, ready to catch me whenever I fell. To feel with certainty that such a safety net existed was
indeed a sweet dream, but one I could not sustain during waking
reality. Not yet.

7

If You See Joy, RUN!

On March 21, 1972 at 1:30 P.M. I found myself at the start of what was becoming a very familiar trip: New York City to 458 West Water Street in Elmira, New York. As I pondered the universe over a bowl of pea soup at the Roscoe Diner (a favorite stopping point for those who traveled Route 17), I hoped that Seth's lack of attendance at last week's class was not going to be repeated tonight.

As class began, discussion centered on the tape recording Jane had played during last week's class concerning her alteration of consciousness experience with the piece of paper. Seth came through early on and informed us that contrary to appearances, or shall I say non-appearances, he was in attendance at last week's class and moreover was aware of each of our reactions as we listened to that tape. Questions came to mind. If Seth was there, where was he? Did he look out into the room from a specific physical point, or is space as we normally think of it irrelevant to the functioning of consciousness?

Also, we are so conditioned to rely exclusively on our outer senses to assess our environment, it never occurred to me during last week's class to try using my inner senses to detect Seth's possible presence. Such an attempt might have yielded some very interesting results. Tonight, however, whatever senses one chose to use, Seth's presence was unmistakable. Referring to the tape recording Jane had played at last week's class, here is part of what Seth had to say:

Many of you ran away from the joy on that tape as you would run away from a murder or an avalanche or an earthquake. Joy will not gobble you up. You will not be lost in it and not be able to find your sorrowful selves again.

Seth's comment about being frightened by joy seemed silly at first, yet a small dose of honest introspection led me to realize that I did indeed have some very limiting ideas about the nature of joy. I wondered where I had picked up such concepts and had a feeling that at least part of the answer would be found in my religious upbringing.

By the time of my Bar Mitzvah (at thirteen years old) I had little interest in religion anymore. Yet religious impressions made upon the young mind have a way of maintaining a presence throughout one's life. The following quote from "Ecclesiastes," one of the books of the Old Testament, typifies the kind of Judeo-Christian attitude toward joy and suffering that would have been a regular part of my early religious training:

"The heart of the wise is in the house of mourning; but the heart of fools is in the house of mirth." We are further instructed to rejoice in our suffering, for suffering was seen as a doorway through which wisdom then emerges. Rejoicing in one's suffering seemed a bit of an oxymoron, yet we were told that God looked with favor upon those who suffered, the state of affliction bearing witness to one's spiritual nature. With such a strong case being built around the benefits of suffering, it's not surprising that such a belief would have become part of my psychic portfolio, one of many limiting beliefs I carried around with me through the years without ever questioning their validity. Once we accept a given belief as true, it often becomes invisible to us. Like a painting that sits on our wall, we walk by it thousands of times, year after year, but no longer notice its lines, or colors, or even the subject matter which fills the frame.

On the way home that evening I had images of cars filled with JOY chasing me down the highway. As I desperately tried to stay ahead of them I wondered what might happen if they were to catch up with me. The scene might have gone something like this:

"This is the JOY PATROL. Pull over—NOW."

I pull over and sit motionless, hands frozen to the steering wheel.

> **JOY PATROL:** "Take your hands off the wheel, slowly, and hand over your license and registration."

With fear coursing through me I follow the officer's instructions. He looks at my license and reads aloud what is written on it: "Sorrowful Self, Negativity Road, State of Despair."

> **JOY PATROL:** "You need to come with us."
>
> **SORROWFUL SELF:** "What did I do wrong? Was I speeding? Did I forget to signal when making a turn?"
>
> **JOY PATROL:** "Oh no, nothing as serious as all that. It's just that your license as a Sorrowful Self has expired and if you want to continue driving you have to reregister as a Joyful Self. There's really no cause for concern. You'll have to appear before the judge, and some minor paperwork is involved, but it's all quite painless."

Upon hearing this news, Sorrowful Self begins to tremble and remains seated in the car, unable to move.

> **JOY PATROL:** "We can do this the easy way or the real easy way, it's up to you. There are no hard ways when it comes to being joyful."

Sorrowful Self goes with the Joy Patrol and appears before the judge. Inside the courtroom the following scene takes place:

JUDGE: "What's the charge?"

OFFICER: "The suspect is being charged with violating sections 34-a through 42-c of the Joyful Code of Existence. Specifically, Mr. Sorrowful Self is being cited for the following:

- Willfully harboring negative expectations on a daily basis.

- Seeing himself as a victim of an unfair and cruel world on numerous occasions.

- Believing suffering is good for the soul and joy is detrimental to one's spiritual growth.

We could go on but in the interests of time we will leave it at that."

JUDGE: "How do you plead?"

SORROWFUL SELF: "GUILTY Your Honor. VERY guilty. TEEMING with guilt."

JUDGE: "You really need to lighten up. Have you ever thought of croquet? It's a wonderful game, very relaxing and yet stimulating at the same time. Before I pass sentence is there anything you would like to say?"

SORROWFUL SELF: "I have one request. Whatever punishment you decide upon, please don't take away ALL my feelings of sorrow. On rainy afternoons I often like to curl up on the couch with a nice big bowl of despair. With each mouthful I savor the melancholy that arises as I think of all the things that have gone wrong in my life, as well as contemplate all the things that can still go wrong in the future. Sometimes as an extra treat I like to sprinkle a few dollops of self-pity on top. If you take away all my feelings of sorrow I think I'd miss such times, so I respectfully request you leave me with at least some feelings of misery."

JUDGE: (turning aside to the clerk and whispering in a sarcastic manner) "Where do they find these people?" He then returns his attention to the defendant.

JUDGE: "Is there anything else?"

SORROWFUL SELF: "Yes, just one more thing. I'd like to know what happens if I refuse to go along with the court's orders. Are you going to slap the cuffs on me and cart me off to jail?"

JUDGE: "Son, you are already in jail, and you are the one handcuffing yourself, not I. So it is entirely up to you what happens, as it always has been. Bask in joy or wallow in sorrow. Live for today or fear tomorrow. I'd love to stay and chat but I have a date to play cribbage. And no offense, but it becomes rather draining being around someone like you. It isn't that you aren't a nice fellow and all that stuff, but your aura just exudes negativity. Dark circles of despair orbit your perimeter. You are like a black hole sucking in great volumes of light and laughter which then disappear inside your gloomy thoughts. I really need to go now but good luck, although luck has nothing to do with it at all."

The judge leaves the courtroom. Sorrowful Self looks at the bailiff who is wearing a tee shirt which has printed on it the words, "Let Us Help You Escape." A poster on the wall with big bright letters contains the following message: "Joy guaranteed in thirty days or a full refund of your misery." Unfortunately, I've chosen the refund far too often. But the good news is that I've been able to arrange for a new hearing to see if at least some of the charges can be dropped. I'm also considering new representation. I'll keep you posted.

The French Connection

It was March 28, 1972, and as they say, spring was just around the corner, but no one had mentioned this to the city of Elmira. Although temperatures dipped below the freezing mark my spirits remained high as once again I sat across from Jane's rocker waiting for that portion of the universe known as Seth to appear. Enter Seth, eyes peering into mine:

> Now: the small but brilliant sardonic part of you was, and in other terms still is, a very brilliant courtesan in 16th century France, who sat with the philosophers and thought they did not know what they were talking about. Since you were a woman with an excellent mind, you listened to these men who seemed to think they knew what they were talking about and you thought, "They do not have the slightest idea in their heads and yet they look at me and think I am beautiful and silly when I can think rings around them." And so you did, and in other terms so you still do. This woman had much energy and still possesses it.

I don't know what prompted Seth to give me this information, and while his comments were certainly intriguing, they didn't spark much of a reaction within me. If I had lived in France during the 16th-century I certainly had no recollection of such a life now. So I filed the information away and continued to grapple with the challenges I was facing in this life, which kept me busy enough.

One day a friend of mine asked me to accompany her to an art exhibit that was displaying the works of René Magritte. Although I am not an art aficionado by any means, I was very taken with Magritte's work and became curious about the man apart from his artwork. So a few days later I went to the New York Public Library in Manhattan, one of the major research facilities in New York City, to learn more about Magritte. I took the appropriate encyclopedia from the shelf, located the entry for René Magritte, and started to read. My attention was suddenly drawn to the opposite page. When I glanced over, staring up at me was the name Marguerite de Valois. There were only a few lines written about her, but one of those lines stated she was "a well-known courtesan in 16th-century France."

Recalling the information that Seth had given me I decided to peruse the library's card catalog to see if there were any references to this Marguerite de Valois person. To my surprise I found quite a few references, one of which mentioned a book Marguerite had written called *Secret and Historic Memoirs of the Courts of France*.

I proceeded to fill out a slip requesting a copy of this book and handed it to the librarian. She told me it would take a few minutes to retrieve since it was located in the archives below the main floor of the library. I imagined the librarian's helper rummaging through stacks of old dust-laden books until finally coming across the title I had requested. It ended up taking about twenty minutes before I had the book in hand. After reading only a few pages I decided that before I started delving any further into this woman's life I wanted to speak with you-know-who.

So at next week's class I asked Seth if he cared to say anything about a "Margaret" de Valois. He paused for a moment, looked at me with an odd expression, and said, *Not now I do not. But I appreciate the reason for the question.* Later, during that same class, he looked at me and said *"Marguerite,"* correcting my earlier mispronunciation when I had said "Margaret." Despite the brevity of Seth's response I knew something was up. Upon returning home I went back to the library and started reading everything I could about Marguerite de Valois. I believe some brief biographical information would be helpful here . . . or dare I say autobiographical.

Marguerite de Valois was born on May 14, 1553. She was the youngest daughter of Henry II of France and Catherine de Medicis. In 1572 a political marriage was arranged between Marguerite and the Protestant Henry of Navarre (later Henry IV). Some years later Marguerite was expelled from the royal court for her political intrigues and in 1586 she was banished to the castle of Usson in Auvergne. In 1599, ten years after Henry of Navarre's accession to the French throne, she consented to the annulment of their marriage. She was subsequently allowed to return to Paris and was granted a stretch of land along the Seine on the Left Bank, where she built a magnificent mansion and lived out her remaining days. Marguerite was admired for her wit and her literary talent. The book I had found at the library containing her memoirs was translated in 1892.

Early on in my research I toyed with the idea of doing an in-depth comparison between Marguerite's life and my own, but I wasn't ready at that point to commit to such an endeavor. Certain similarities, however, became readily apparent. The list below contains only a few examples of many parallels I found between Marguerite and myself.

- Marguerite had a habit of holding a pen in her hand whenever she was reading a book. I have that same habit.
- Marguerite had a passion for philosophy and wanted to open a school where philosophy could be studied. While attending Jane's classes I often thought how wonderful it would be to have a school or center where people could get together and explore Seth's ideas.
- Marguerite loved dancing. As a teenager I loved to dance, although I'm sure my gyrations would have raised more than a few royal eyebrows had they taken place on the palace floor in France.

The following connection I found particularly intriguing:

- Marguerite composed light melodies on her lute for various psalms and hired singers to perform her arrangements. I compose simple melodies on my guitar and like Marguerite have hired singers at times to perform some of my compositions.
- Marguerite developed a passion for gardening late in life. In my fifties, for the first time in my life I also developed a passion for gardening. Despite having worked all week, I would often get up early on a Saturday morning and work in the garden until well into the afternoon.

Besides discovering various traits we had in common, we shared certain personality characteristics as well as dealing with similar challenges, although the outer circumstances of course differed. Throughout our lives we had great difficulty with figures of authority, which when combined with a very stubborn nature often led to many conflicts, in particular with our respective mothers. Issues having to do with betrayal by friends and lovers also figured prominently in both our lives. Another shared element was a tendency toward violence, although I like to think I've worked that one out to a great degree in this life.

There were also instances where events would seem to overlap. For example I would read about an event in Marguerite's life, and then either that same day or shortly thereafter, a parallel event would occur in my own life. The following are but two examples. One day I was reading about a period in Marguerite's life when the court set up residence in the city of Navarre. As I left the library that day and was walking around Manhattan I passed by a hotel called Hotel Navarre. During all my years of traversing the city I could not recall having passed by this hotel before.

Another incident occurred when I was reading about one of Marguerite's first love affairs. She was in love with a well-known military leader named the Duke d'Guise, and believing the feelings to be mutual was quite surprised when the Duke informed her one day that he had proposed to another and his proposal had been accepted. The day after reading about this, I was speaking with a woman I had grown increasingly fond of, and believing the feelings to be mutual, I was quite surprised when she informed me that a friend of ours had proposed to her and she had happily accepted his proposal.

As I became further immersed in my study of Marguerite's life and times I began to get feelings about various people I knew in this life and who they were in the context of 16th-century France. For example, I had the distinct feeling that my friend Rick Stack was this Duke d'Guise fellow I had just spoken of. The more I read about the Duke d'Guise the more I began to see connections between Rick and the Duke.

One day while Rick and I were in the middle of an argument, he used the phrase, "You stabbed me in the back." There was something about the phrase itself and the way he said it that seemed peculiar. I later found out as part of my research that in 1563 the Duke d'Guise was summoned to the Château de Blois, ostensibly to meet with King Henry III (who was Marguerite's brother). As the Duke awaited the king's presence a band of assassins hired by the king was hiding in the shadows. They snuck up behind the Duke and repeatedly stabbed him in the back, the wounds proving to be fatal.

After many hours and months of research I reached a point where I became determined to get verification from Seth that Marguerite de Valois was the woman Seth had been referring to when he gave me that reincarnational data about 16th-century France. Here is part of the exchange that took place between us one evening in Jane's living room.

> RICH: Just one question in my thick skull I want to know for sure—is Marguerite de Valois the woman you were referring to when you gave me that information?
> SETH: *It is indeed.*
> RICH: Thank you. You have made me feel outrageous.
> SETH: *No, you have made yourself feel outrageous. When you told your story just now, you wondered whether you had been that woman. It is quite as proper of course, to say that woman was*

you. It is much more basically truthful to say that a correspondence exists between you and that woman now; but you are yourself now and not the woman.

As the years went by I spent less and less time thinking about Marguerite de Valois, yet reincarnational selves, like long lost relatives, have a way of turning up when you least expect them. In 1990 my friend Leslie and I were vacationing in Bolton Landing, a town in upstate New York about ten miles from Lake George. One of the tourist brochures had listed a local attraction called The Madame Sembrich Museum. Neither Leslie nor I had the slightest idea who this Madame Sembrich was, yet Leslie was insistent that we go. I decided what the heck, since we didn't have anything else planned for the day. The "museum" was actually a small house where Madame Sembrich used to live. We learned that Madame Sembrich was a famous opera singer in the late 19th century, and the house was filled with miscellaneous memorabilia from her career. Among the items on display were some of the original gowns she had worn while appearing in various operas. A small card next to each gown listed the name of the opera as well as the operatic character she had portrayed. I suddenly noticed the word Huguenots written on one of the cards. The Huguenots were the French Protestants who were at the center of the religious wars that raged in France during much of the 16th century. The card stated that this particular gown was worn by Madame Sembrich in the opera "The Huguenots," during her portrayal of—Marguerite de Valois.

Another unexpected reminder of Marguerite's existence occurred toward the end of 1994 as the result of a phone call I received from friend and compatriot Sue Watkins. (Sue is the author of *Conversations with Seth*.) Sue called to let me know that she had just read a movie review of a film entitled *Queen Margo*, based on the life of Marguerite de Valois. The film, by the way, was nominated for numerous awards and received an Academy Award nomination in the category of "Best Costume Design." (I think Marguerite would have been pleased by this as she was known in her day for having introduced many new fashions to France.)

One last connection—last for the moment, for I don't think connections ever really end. In *Dreams, "Evolution," And Value Fulfillment,* one of the Seth books, Seth makes reference to a private session he held for Jane and Rob in March of 1981. During this session Seth spoke of how Jane had initiated a small religious order—in 16th-century France!

I believe reincarnational selves speak to us every day in various guises and that there are always clues for us to follow. When we are open to such possibilities we need not search for those selves; they will find us. So the next time a stranger comes knocking at the door of your consciousness or starts ringing the bell, do yourself a favor; let them in.

9

Go West, Young Man

As the warm winds of May began their march across the countryside, the last remnants of snow and ice that had been holding
their ground finally gave up the fight. With my twenty second birth-
day coming up I realized how my feelings about life had changed.
I wouldn't say I had become bitter, but certainly disillusioned. My
faith in the universe had definitely taken a beating. Jane began class
by presenting us with the following choice: either tell a secret or
talk about our self-image and how we might want to change it. The
self-image option brought forth an immediate sense of queasiness,
so I opted for the telling of a secret. I picked a secret that didn't hold
much of a charge for me, disclosing the fact that at nineteen years
old I had become involved with shooting heroin.

Unlike other drugs I had experimented with in the 1960s, my
involvement with heroin thrust me inside of a dangerous game,
and while I tried to tell myself I had the upper hand, in truth, my
"opponent" was growing stronger every time we met. Heroin's sweet
embrace was insidiously tightening its grip upon me. I realized that
if I continued in the same vein (pun intended), I was going to end up
either dead or in jail, neither of them very attractive choices. I needed

to get away. A change of scenery was essential. The only question was where to go. For a nineteen-year old hippie with shoulder-length hair in 1969, California seemed like the obvious choice.

So I got up early one summer morning, grabbed my duffle bag, hastily stuffed some clothes inside of it, and headed toward the door. I paused for a few moments and thought of my mother who lay sleeping in the next room. She had been through some pretty rough times with me, and all things considered it just seemed best to let her sleep. I quietly shut the door, walked to a nearby intersection, and in typical hitchhiker fashion put my thumb in the air. So began my west coast pilgrimage. Whenever anyone stopped and inquired as to where I was headed, I just asked if they were going in a westerly direction; if the answer was yes, I'd hop in.

I received a number of rides that first day and as night descended I found myself near a town called Bentleyville, Pennsylvania. I was starting to get tired and made camp for the night on a large area of grass alongside the highway. I then fell into a light sleep and was awoken by the reflection of some lights ahead of me. A car was backing up and heading right toward me. As the car stopped I heard a voice call out, "Are you okay?" I walked over to the car and found two guys sitting in the front seat. I told them I was hitchhiking to California. Talk about serendipity: they just happened to be on their way to Los Angeles. They were going to drive straight through with each of them taking turns driving while the other one slept. No motels for these guys, and that was fine with me.

What was also fine with me was that they paid for every one of my meals, and when we stopped in Las Vegas they even gave me money to bet with. They never once asked for anything in return.

Before this trip I hadn't ventured very far from New York, and as we made our way across the country I was struck by the beauty of the United States. Images such as the Rocky Mountains, the brilliant red sandstone structures of Utah, the tranquility of the Pacific Ocean—all these sights and more began to trigger within me a sense of wonder I hadn't felt in a long time. And having only seen pictures of surfing on television, watching real live surfers ride the waves off the coast of Malibu is a memory I'll never forget.

As I think about the two guys who picked me up that night in Pennsylvania, I'm reminded of how total strangers will sometimes provide us with exactly the kind of assistance we need at a particular juncture in our lives. Although years later neither of us may be able to recall each other's names or faces, for a brief time these strangers become part of our journey and we become a part of theirs.

Getting back to class and the sharing of secrets, others were far more courageous than I was that evening. Some spoke of events that had happened many years before, yet the emotional intensity with which they related those events made it seem as if they had occurred just yesterday. As the evening progressed I thought about secrets and why they exist.

Through the centuries the human race has not been held in very high esteem, to say the least. Our very existence on earth is often seen as compelling evidence that we have fallen out of grace with God. If you asked mass consciousness for a definition of "human being," it might read as follows: "A human being is a creature that is inherently flawed, born in sin, and filled with dark thoughts and destructive impulses." With such beliefs as a backdrop, not being open with others is quite understandable, for in being open we just might inadvertently reveal something about ourselves that supports this idea that to be human means to be part of an inferior and tainted race.

How different, and delightfully so, were Seth's sentiments along these lines. Over and over again Seth spoke of the innocence of our being, maintaining that we were not creatures born in sin and thus our souls did not need saving. Furthermore, Seth asserted that whatever we did—or didn't do—we could not fall out of grace with God. Now those are the types of messages I'd love to hear preached from the pulpits on Sunday mornings. But mass consciousness doesn't seem ready to deliver sermons espousing the proposition that our beings are naturally good, so if we want to hear such sermons, I think for now we'll have to preach them to ourselves.

10

Back At The Parade

On the way up to class this particular day, I started thinking about how week after week we'd pass through the same towns, go by the same houses, yet I'd probably never have a chance to meet with or talk to any of the occupants. But I wondered: how many of those people had the same need I did to try to understand the way reality worked? Was I better off for having such a need, or was my quest symptomatic of a maladjusted consciousness, unable to enjoy life without mentally dissecting it to pieces? I remembered how my mother used to say to me, "Richard, you think too much." Maybe she was right. Why couldn't I be at peace with the mysteries that surrounded me, be content with my unknowing?

That night in class when I had mentioned the fact that as a teenager I had become involved with taking heroin, one of the students asked me what I was trying to escape. Before I had a chance to answer, Seth came through and said: *He was trying to escape the burden of consciousness; the burden of questions that seemingly come without end and without answer.*

Seth's comment about questions that "come without end and without answer" was a valid description of how I often felt. It was like going to a parade every day, but this was not like any parade you have been to before. In this parade, the floats were composed of thousands of questions marks, all of which would light up at the same time as the floats would pass by. Although almost blinded by the light, I would just stand there staring, unable to divert my eyes, locked in some kind of hypnotic trance that I did not know how to break.

The floats would then be followed by the marching bands. With each beat of the drum or sound of the trumpet a new question mark would be released into the air, all of them then coming together to form this huge cloud in the shape of one big question mark, which hovered over the entire parade route. Off to the side jugglers would be competing to see how many question marks they could keep suspended in the air at the same time without having any hit the ground.

But the contortionists were the ones that always affected me the most. Their bodies were bent into grotesque shapes, tied up in knots from all the unanswered questions that had been living inside of them for years, the deformity of muscle and bone so pronounced that there was no way to hide the pain they were in. They would always walk in single file, and when they reached the spot where I was standing, each one would turn and look at me, and I could see the hope in their eyes that I just might be the one, like Neo in *The Matrix,* who could finally set them free. Yet all I could do was stand there, a silent spectator, and watch their inevitable disappointment as they realized I was in no less need of help than they were.

Eventually the parade would end, and everyone would make their way home, their attention drawn to the mundane details of everyday life. But as tomorrow would arrive, we'd all find ourselves back at the parade, the same scenes being repeated with little variation. Yet I often asked myself: Did it have to begin again? Wouldn't it be so much easier to forget all these questions and just get on with my life, doing the best I could with whatever knowledge I had already attained? I think in many ways it would be easier, and for short periods of time I was able to live that way, to stop trying to figure out the big picture and just take care of whatever tasks I needed to perform to get me through each day.

But such periods never lasted long. It would only take some minor event or some stray thought to start my mind going in a certain direction, and before I knew it I'd be back at the parade.

Talking about question marks, there was one that had started out as a tiny seed but had now grown into a huge tree, its branches spreading out to every corner of Jane's living room, pushing up against those bay windows as if ready to crash through them at any moment. That question mark was asking whether it was possible for me to still continue following Marcel's philosophy when it had become apparent that the basic tenets upon which it rested were diametrically opposed to the ideas being presented by Jane and Seth. This was no minor disagreement over some esoteric point or wrangling over how many angels could dance on the head of a pin. As but one example, here's an excerpt from a letter Marcel wrote to Jane in 1970.

> Dear Miss Roberts:
> Your book [*The Seth Material*] is an excellent one, but dangerous for the layman. The world inside of us is far more powerful than a billion hydrogen bombs. Dreams are not to be toyed with by the unknowledgeable. There are the most horrendous beasts, demons and ogres there.

Contrast that with Seth's continued encouragement to explore the dream state without any hesitation or fear, and you can see how the two philosophies had a very different view of the universe. This conflict had been growing within me for a number of months and was now reaching a critical mass. Something had to give, and I could feel both sides starting to dig in their heels. You may have heard the expression, "This town isn't big enough for the both of us." Well, in this case my psyche wasn't big enough to play host to two opposing belief systems. For the moment, guns remained in their holsters—but the showdown was inevitable.

11

Number 2 Must Try Harder

In many ways it was a typical Tuesday afternoon, although I'm not sure "typical" is an apt description for driving two hundred forty miles to hear some woman speak in trance and then driving back that same night.

An October sky was wavering between various shades of grey as if it couldn't make up its mind whether it was going to remain overcast or let some sunshine in. My mood was also wavering, as one moment I'd be feeling relatively calm, and then the next moment I'd be experiencing this growing sense of anxiousness. By the time we stopped for lunch I found myself standing outside the Roscoe Diner in the middle of a full-blown anxiety attack. I told Jeff I was going to hitch back to New York City and that he should continue on to class without me. Although neither of us knew what was behind the angst I was feeling, Jeff was finally able to help me calm down. By the time we arrived in Elmira, the whole incident had been relegated to the background of my consciousness.

As class began I took my usual place on the floor not far from Jane's rocker, and it wasn't long before Seth came through. He started speaking about beliefs, and how beliefs influence our experience not only in waking reality but in the dream state as well. There was then this long pause. An uneasy sensation in the pit of my stomach began to form. Finally, Seth broke the silence:

Number 2 must try harder, and Number 3 must try harder still.

Although Seth's comment was rather cryptic, I was sure it didn't refer to the Avis Rent-A-Car Company, which in 1962 adopted the slogan "We Try Harder."

What I felt it did refer to was "Richard Kendall's Spiritual Rankings," a guru rating service to which I was the only subscriber. Coming in at Number 1, and holding on to that ranking for over a year (despite the fact that he was dead) was Marcel. And although Seth was edging up in the standings every week he still remained at Number 2. Lagging behind both of them was Jane at Number 3.

Prior to this evening Seth had not so much as taken a jab at Marcel, but tonight Seth wasn't pulling any punches. He zeroed in on what he saw as major flaws in Marcel's teachings as well as the teaching methods themselves, which in Seth's opinion left much to be desired.

Seth continued to pick apart Marcel's world view as skillfully as a professional boxer might pick apart his opponent in the middle of the ring. But for Seth this wasn't a competition or a desire to move up in "the rankings." The only place where any kind of competition actually existed was in the arena of my own mind, where two opposing belief systems had been vying for dominance, and tonight, one of them was going to fall hard (something I had picked up on during the car ride to class, hence my feelings of anxiousness and inexplicable behavior).

I also think the timing on Seth's part as to when to address this whole issue was far from accidental. If Seth had criticized Marcel or his teachings when we first started attending classes, it's possible we may not have returned, for sometimes in trying to get someone to look at something they are not ready to face, you end up just pushing them further away. I think Seth had been acutely aware of all these issues and knew when the time would be right for him to speak out, and that time was tonight.

Marcel had been sitting in the middle of my psyche with a presence larger than life for over two years. Firmly planted in his kingly chair, he was lord and master over all he surveyed. But as Seth spoke tonight, that chair began to rock back and forth. It then started to shake violently, and although Marcel tried valiantly to hold on, he just couldn't do so any longer. He was thrown high into the air and came crashing down with a very loud and unceremonious thud.

A huge hole then opened up in the roof of Jane's apartment. Marcel's body was sucked up right through that hole, went shooting through the clouds, and in a matter of moments disappeared completely from view. All that was left was this large empty chair that Marcel had once sat in.

"Who will sit in this chair next?" I wondered. The obvious answer was Seth, except for one very important point: Seth had no interest in playing the guru game or being set up as an icon in anyone's psyche. There was only one person Seth was interested in having us set up as "Number 1" in our psyche, and that was ourselves.

Jane also had no interest in the guru game and was much too savvy to let herself fall into that kind of a trap. Jane once told us she could have had many of us totally wrapped around her finger if she wanted to, and I don't doubt that for a second. But she also said that one of her challenges in this life was to not use her energy in such a manner, and I'd say she met that challenge beautifully.

Jane knew that with the slightest encouragement from her, others would have all too willingly forsaken their own sense of self, looking to Jane and Seth for all their answers. Many (including myself) were already leaning in that direction. Her purpose as a teacher was not to magnify her own persona at the expense of her students but to lead each of us back to our own sense of power; to inspire within each of us the confidence to look for our own answers; and to trust the authority of our own psyche. Over the years my appreciation of Jane grew considerably, realizing that she was far more than just a conduit for Seth to come through.

At one point during the evening I found myself thinking: "As soon as I get home I'm going to sell every one of those books that Marcel had insisted we buy as part of his required reading list." I then pulled back in my mind, thinking that acting in such a manner might be a bit rash. At that very moment Seth looked at me and said *And do not worry about the angle at which you are leaning any more than a flower does.* (A few days later I did sell every one of those books and boy, did that feel good.)

As I remember that evening when the "Marcel trance" was broken, I can better appreciate the difficulty people have when trying to break away from frameworks they have navigated within for long periods of time. The framework can take any number of forms, such as a relationship, a religion, a career, or a strong belief that has dominated one's world view for many years. And lest I portray myself as too brave, when I finally decided to break with Marcel's teachings, I did have Jane's classes as a backup.

Yet there are times in people's lives when every fiber of their being is screaming out for change and yet no visible backup awaits them. During such times, taking that first step can be terrifying as one feels like they are walking off a cliff blindfolded. Faced with such fear, there is often a strong tendency to cling tightly to that which is familiar.

Yet when we find the courage to leave the old behind, to take that leap of faith, our world begins again. Space itself—psychological space, that is—literally expands, making room for events and experiences that could not have materialized within the confines of the old framework. And despite our fears we do land on safe ground, although it may take a little time to acclimate ourselves to our new surroundings.

Before this chapter draws to a close I want to mention something Seth said that night regarding Marcel. Before we went to Jane's classes we asked Marcel for his permission to go. I can't speak for anyone else, but I was so deeply under Marcel's spell at the time that had he said it was not a good idea, I probably wouldn't have gone. Fortunately, he did give his consent. Regarding this point Seth made the following comment: *He [Marcel] well knew what would happen when he acquiesced to you coming here, and he did that for you. And do not forget it.*

I have not forgotten, so let me say this: "Thank you, Marcel, for the generosity of spirit that allowed you to acquiesce to my going to Jane's classes. And if our paths cross again, let us not meet as master and disciple but greet each other as equals, and in so doing we will be honoring ourselves and honoring each other."

But let's not meet *too* soon. I have miles to go before I sleep—two hundred forty to be exact!"

12

Birds Flying High

I hadn't been to class in a few weeks but in the interim had read a small book that knocked my proverbial socks off. The name of the book was *Jonathan Livingston Seagull,* by Richard Bach. First published in 1970, by the end of 1972 over a million copies were in print and the book reached the top of the *New York Times* Best Seller list where it remained for thirty-eight weeks.

As the story goes, late one night Dick Bach was walking along the beach when he heard a voice say "Jonathan Livingston Seagull." He turned around but no one was there. When he returned home the voice came to him again and started dictating what became the text of the book. The voice then stopped, and when Bach tried to finish the book "on his own" he couldn't. Years later the voice spontaneously returned and the book was finished.

As I reached the doorway of 458 West Water Street I bounded up the stairs, eager to share my discovery of this book with Jane and the rest of the class. Everyone including Jane was already seated and class was about to begin. But before taking my seat I stopped by Jane's rocker, and with great enthusiasm started telling her about this wonderful book I had just read called *Jonathan Livingston Seagull.*

Jane listened patiently, and when I was finished she pointed to the couch and said, "Rich, meet Dick Bach."

Dick Bach received a lot of attention that night from Seth as visitors often did, whether famous or not. Sumari came through with a song enacting a drama involving Dick Bach and two other class members. It seemed that all three of them knew each other in another life and also knew "Nebene," a reincarnational aspect of Rob Butts. After the song ended there was general discussion about the subject of reincarnation. As I was trying to unravel ideas such as simultaneous time and the past having its own past, present, and future, Seth joined the conversation speaking directly to me:

If you want to understand what reincarnation is, then examine this instant of your being. From this moment, as you understand it, all realities flow and are created. As I was writing this chapter and reviewing Seth's words about reincarnation, I took a break and turned on the television. Flashing across the screen was an advertisement for a movie called *Mongol,* set to open in theaters later in the month. The movie explored the early life of Genghis Khan, who was born in Mongolia around 1162. A brutal but effective military leader, Genghis Khan created an empire that included parts of China, Central Asia, the Middle East, and Europe.

As I watched the trailer for *Mongol* I was reminded of a dream I had had years earlier. In this dream I was in a room with Jane Roberts. Jane and I sat facing each other when suddenly her entire visage began to change. I watched in amazement as Jane transformed into this very fierce looking Mongolian warrior with sword in hand, muscular physique, and thick mustache. I could feel the intense energy that surrounded this man. I just stared at him without speaking a word and he stared right back at me, also without speaking a word. I finally said, "Jane, one of your incarnations is showing." This warrior then transformed back into Jane, who said to me with a smile, "No, Rich, it's one of yours!" I promptly woke up and to this day I clearly remember the image of that warrior.

As far as Genghis Kahn is concerned, I do not believe he was a past self of mine, nor do I feel any particular connection with Genghis Kahn himself. But I do feel that the dream had validity and that it is important for me to be open to the possibility that there was a self of mine who lived during the era in which Genghis Kahn ruled.

Remembering this dream also led me to think about some of the implications of reincarnation when viewed in the light of various ideas put forth by Seth and Jane. If we consider identity as a gestalt, a functioning unit comprised of numerous aspects or selves, each equally alive in their own respective time periods, with no real separation between them, then the thoughts, feelings, and experiences of one aspect would be available to all the other aspects that together form one's overall entity.

On some level, not only would each aspect be aware of the experiences of all the other aspects, but at times personality characteristics belonging to those other selves might momentarily "intrude" into what we think of as *our* time frame, as we find ourselves reacting to an event or something that someone says in a very uncharacteristic manner. (I put the word "intrude" in quotes because there is no trespass here; on some level we would have acquiesced to the experience.) Jane used to call such events "bleedthroughs."

As an example, let's assume that the Mongolian warrior who appeared in my dream is an aspect of my being. Let's also assume that one day I was feeling very angry at someone. Normally, I might imagine myself yelling at this other person, or writing them a nasty letter. But what if instead I found myself visualizing what it would be like to commit an act of extreme violence against this person and feeling a great sense of satisfaction as this violent scene played out in my mind.

During the time I was entertaining such thoughts they would have felt quite natural, yet afterwards I might have been appalled at having imagined such things. Yet for my Mongolian warrior, from whom I "borrowed" such violent musings, those thoughts would have not seemed odd at all. They would have fit right in with his overall view of the world at the time.

Seth stated numerous times that all divisions between selves are illusory, nothing more than artificial constructs designed to allow us to operate comfortably within our own particular time period. So if we removed the illusion of time, what would serve as a dividing element between selves, allowing us to distinguish one from the other. In a painting, although the colors may bleed into each other, there is enough of a contrast not to mistake, let's say, blue for red. Yet at the same time, if the painting were viewed under a high-powered microscope, one would be hard-pressed to identify an exact point where one color ended and another began. I think within the overall psychic structure of our being the same concept applies. Using my Mongolian warrior as an example, there would be no *precise point* where he ended and I began, and vice versa. Carrying this analogy forward to Jane's relationship with Seth, if Seth and Jane are part of the same entity, which Seth stated early on in the sessions, there would also be no precise point where Jane Roberts ended and Seth began, and again, vice versa. From that standpoint, within the multidimensional personality structure of Jane, Seth in certain terms would always be present. Here are some of Jane's thoughts regarding the nature of her relationship with Seth:

> *Spirit guide terminology is completely inaccurate to explain*
> *personalities such as Seth, and any of the same kind that you*
> *might encounter as a result of your own experience. I do not believe*
> *they are spirits in the terms meant. I consider the Seth material*
> *as evidence of other Aspects of the multidimensional personality.*
> *Would a Seth experiencing Jane think of her as a lesser developed*
> *personality. Maybe; but just maybe he'd also think of her as one*
> *with great growing potential to be encouraged, so that in time*
> *terms he with his ability could emerge. He would be me in my*
> *present time, developing abilities that would later let him be him.*
> *And simultaneously I would be developed. And simultaneously*
> *I would be him developing and guiding me in my present time.*
> *The usual spirit interpretation isn't a step ahead of the normal*
> *psychological explanation at all because they automatically take*
> *it for granted that the guide is outside ourselves or independent,*
> *because inside or coexistent sounds awful and means it's just you.*

I believe that when Jane was transmitting information from Seth, we'd be witnessing a "bleedthrough" of major proportions, as

Jane's and Seth's consciousnesses would in some way temporarily merge, resulting in the personality structure we then called Seth. But the resulting personality structure that was visible to us when Jane spoke for Seth would represent only a small portion of Seth's (as well as Jane's) greater reality.

And couldn't the same be said about all of us—that the self we know in physical reality, the part that is visible to ourselves and to others, represents only a small portion of our true identity when we take into account all of the various aspects that are alive within our psyche right now, although on a daily basis we are normally unaware of their presence or activities. We often block ourselves from becoming aware of other aspects because we fear such an awareness might threaten our sense of identity. Yet I think that the opposite holds true—that an awareness of other aspects within one's being doesn't weaken one's sense of identity but strengthens it.

Jane's abilities were quite remarkable in that not only was she able to become consciously aware of another aspect of her own being but also was able to consistently give expression to that aspect for over twenty years, bringing back to this reality, in a coherent and creative manner, knowledge that was beyond what "Jane" possessed "on her own."

While many of us do not have the spontaneous inclination toward the kind of mediumship Jane was involved with (and there's no reason why we should) the abilities behind such phenomena belong to all of us. They are natural attributes of consciousness.

I think the more we trust the nature of the self, the more we will automatically utilize abilities of consciousness that we normally inhibit without even realizing we are doing so. For example, I think it would be quite natural at times to look out at the world through the eyes of others and in the process acquire deeper levels of understanding and empathy, not only in relation to those others but also in relation to ourselves. My friend Emmy van Swaaij from the Netherlands often has dreams where she finds herself "peeking along" through the eyes of others, but there's no reason why we couldn't do the same in waking reality.

Returning to my Mongolian warrior, I am going to take a few

moments and send him images of peace and thoughts of nonviolence. I'm going to suggest that he throw away his sword, invite his enemies to sit with him at his table, and offer them a bottle of kumis as a token of friendship. He may ask himself where such strange thoughts come from, and if I answered him by saying that they originated from within himself there would be much truth to that statement. But to say such a statement represented "the truth, the whole truth, and nothing but the truth" would put me at risk of perjury. And Mongolian warriors have their own ways of dealing with those who lie to them. Trust me, you don't want to know.

13

SO FARUNDE DE BADETA LE ORLE A TO MAR LON TOR FAR-ATA

Every so often I would come up to Elmira a few days before class and stay with an old friend who had moved to the Elmira area. One week I took advantage of such an opportunity, arriving on a Thursday afternoon. With class not scheduled to begin until Tuesday, I had plenty of time to relax. I then remembered that on Friday nights Jane and Rob often had informal gatherings at their apartment. I called and asked if I could join them and was given the okay. Besides myself, only a few other people showed up, none of them regular class members. These were meant to be social occasions with Seth rarely coming through.

At some point in that evening I mentioned that I wasn't working at the moment and, in a casual manner, added the fact that I had gone on welfare to help me get by. Not having a job was one thing, but my comment about being on welfare really pushed Jane's buttons. For Jane, being on welfare was not some minor footnote one alludes to with the same nonchalance one might comment about some movie they recently saw. Jane's parents had split up when Jane was three years old, and with her father taking off for California and her mother bedridden with rheumatoid arthritis, welfare was the only way they were able to survive.

After expressing her anger and displeasure in response to what I had just disclosed, informal gathering or not, Jane went into a Sumari trance. This time, however, instead of singing or speaking in Sumari, she wrote down the following Sumari words on a piece of paper: SO FARUNDE DE BADETA LE ORLE A TO MAR LON TOR FAR-ATA. On that same piece of paper she then wrote down the English translation: "The bread is stolen from the seagulls." As she handed me that piece of paper it was obvious that what I thought was going to be an innocent little get-together was turning out to be not so innocent after all.

As the evening progressed, Jane started reading some of the correspondence she had recently received. Since the publication of her book *The Seth Material,* a steady stream of letters had arrived at Jane's doorstep. Written by people from all walks of life, some letters were simply expressions of gratitude for the work she and Rob were doing, while many others contained requests for help from either Jane or Seth or both.

One of the letters she read that evening was from a nun who was discussing masturbation. Jane picked up that I was having a reaction to this letter and asked me what was up. What I really wanted to say was that I just remembered I had a very important appointment in town and had to leave right away, if not sooner. But we can never really outrun the contents of our own consciousness.

I explained that my reaction had less to do with the subject matter of the letter than the fact that for some reason it triggered a very unpleasant memory within me. Without going into any details I simply stated that when I was fifteen years old I had been raped.

Hardly a word was spoken in response to what I had just revealed, either by Jane, or the other folks present. As the night ended I figured that was the end of the story. Oh how naïve we can be...

14

There Is Someone
In This Room

After having spent the last few days hanging out with my friend in Elmira, today was Tuesday, and if it was Tuesday, it was class night. What a pleasure it was to be able to walk over to Jane's house as opposed to the long drive from New York City, which despite the pleasant scenery could be rather tedious at times. During class the subject of secrets came up. "There is someone in this room who has a secret that if told will help someone else in this room." Jane spoke these words while staring straight ahead, her eyes not resting upon anyone. She waited a few moments, and after receiving no response, she repeated the same statement once more: "There is someone in this room who has a secret that if told will help someone else in this room." Again, no response. No one seemed to have the slightest inkling as to what Jane was referring to—no one, that was, except me. As my vocal chords began to tighten I knew the secret Jane was referring to was my having been raped, which I had mentioned a few days earlier at that Friday night get-together. In the words of my dear departed grandmother: "Oy vey." To speak of this event in front of all my buddies as well as all the other people present in the room that evening was something I was not eager to do.

Because of the kind of atmosphere that existed in Jane's class, one often felt more comfortable revealing things about themselves in that room than anywhere else on earth; yet I still had mixed feelings as to whether to proceed or not. I finally decided to go ahead and let the chips fall where they may.

After I finished speaking, one of the women in class started to cry softly. She then told of how she was sexually abused by her father as a child. Suddenly, it was as if some kind of invisible floodgate opened up, and what came pouring out was a veritable potpourri of sexual secrets, as people began to share details about sexual experiences that had occurred in their lives of which they had never spoken before. As this deluge of repressed memories continued to inundate the room (in some cases these memories had been buried for decades) one of my friends spontaneously announced that he was gay. While this had been a source of speculation in the past, for him to volunteer that information in class took a lot of guts.

When all was said and done and the dust finally settled, we sat in a room littered with "dirty" little (and in some cases *big*) secrets, but we all survived. Actually, there wasn't one negative or judgmental response to anything that was divulged that evening. As for me, I was relieved to have finally released a secret I had harbored for a very long time.

Some people say let sleeping dogs lie. Yet sometimes, the simple act of sharing something that you have never been able to talk about before can be a very freeing experience. Perhaps in sharing the details of what happened to me, someone else may feel inclined to share an event in their own life (of whatever nature) that until now they have never been able to disclose.

When I was fifteen years old I used to hang out in Greenwich Village in New York City. In the early 1960s this part of the city attracted various groups of people who felt that they did not fit in with mainstream society, many of them openly challenging the values and traditions that America had been built upon. So here I am one evening sitting alone on a bench in Washington Square Park, a well-known park in the middle of Greenwich Village, thinking that

I had some kind of street smarts and could handle anything that might come my way. This black man then appears out of nowhere, sits down next to me, and offers to share his bottle of wine with me. I readily accept and it wasn't long before the world began to take on a much rosier glow. He then suggested we continue the festivities back at his apartment. Even in the semi-inebriated state I had slid into, something told me that this invitation had strings attached to it, but not listening to that little voice inside my head I got into a taxi with him and off we went. We ended up in a part of the city I wasn't very familiar with, and after being in his apartment for only a short time he began to come on to me.

Being fifteen years old and a virgin as far as heterosexual *or* homosexual sex was concerned, I started to get pretty damn nervous. I told him I wanted to leave and go back to Greenwich Village. He said that was fine and he would go back with me but first he needed to get something from the bedroom. A few moments later he returned from the bedroom, walked up to me, and in one smooth motion took out from behind his back this humongous butcher knife —which was now resting an inch from my throat. He then stared at me with the coldest eyes I have ever seen. "Take off your clothes," he commanded. I refused. With the knife now held right against my neck he proclaimed, "I'm not jiving with you, take off your clothes, right now!" I knew this was no idle threat. I took off my clothes and he proceeded to repeatedly rape me in a most painful manner. The knife sat silently by the edge of the bed, ready to pounce should it detect any movement on my part to escape.

When he was done, he told me he had to run some errands but that he loved me so much he couldn't bear to think of me leaving him, so it was best that he chain me to the bed. Somehow I was able to find enough presence of mind to convince him that I loved him too, and there was no need to chain me to the bed, and that I would gladly be there when he returned. After he left the apartment I waited a few minutes and then bolted for the door. Once outside I started running and running with tears streaming down my face. I finally came across a train station and eventually made my way back to my parents' house in Queens, New York. I can't even imagine how my parents would have reacted had I told them what I had just been through. I went to my room and tried to sleep.

As the days progressed I struggled mightily with feelings I couldn't identify, much less manage. If I was riding on a train or a bus and the man sitting next to me would even slightly brush up against me with his elbow or arm, I would start feeling this intense anger. This would then be followed by feelings of extreme mental anguish that I had no idea how to deal with. It took a long time before I began to understand that the anger and the pain were being driven in large part by a deep sense of shame for what had happened to me.

Perhaps if I had gone to some counselor trained in such things they would have pointed that out to me from the beginning, but until that Friday night get-together at Jane's, and then in class a few days later, I wasn't able to reveal to anyone what had happened to me. Looking back at that event from the standpoint of my present consciousness, I am able to recognize (and acknowledge) the part I played in its creation. This is not to say that I consciously knew exactly the way things were going to unfold, but to feign total innocence would be a lie. At that time in my life I was feeling conflicted about my sexuality. While I was for the most part drawn to women, there was a part of me that wanted to experience sex with a man. I wouldn't admit that to myself on a conscious level, much less bring myself to willingly seek such an encounter. So my "solution" was to create a situation where I would be forced into having such an experience—a poor solution for sure.

There was also a detail that occurred that evening which even then I sensed had a certain significance to it, although at the time I had no frame of reference from which to explore it. The detail I'm referring to occurred in this man's apartment when at some point in the evening I asked him his name. He paused for a few moments, as if he was searching for exactly the right way to answer my question, and then said, "Just call me Justice." Looking at that statement now, with a greater awareness of the way realities mix and merge, I am reminded of the first class I attended at Jane's house. As you may recall, I was involved in a reincarnational drama where I was supposed to have been a judge presiding over a trial where Ray, one of the students in class, was accused (in that lifetime) of committing a sexually immoral act. That judge, being responsible for deciding appropriate sentences for various crimes, would have been involved on a daily basis with issues regarding justice.

In the case of Ray, that judge felt justice was best served by handing out a severe sentence. Yet if, as Seth maintains, the past is not a done and finished product, then a change of beliefs in the present could significantly affect events from our past. According to Seth, this would not simply be a symbolic change but a literal changing of the past.

This led me to wonder: when Ray and I made peace that evening, standing alongside Jane with our hands clasped together, could those hands have reached back into the past, prompting that judge to hand out a far more compassionate and lenient sentence, creating a "new" version of the past that was just as valid as the "old" one? Did this new version replace the old version, or did both versions exist alongside each other with one becoming the new "official" version? Would the experience I had with "Justice" in *my* present, affect that judge in *his* present, perhaps leading him to reexamine his ideas about justice in general? And going back to Ray for a moment, he just happens to be gay in this life, adding another evocative element to the whole drama.

Whatever the answers to these questions might be, I could no longer pack events into a neat little box, slap a label on them with a specific beginning and ending date, and tuck them away in some corner never to be opened again. Seth has said that we actually change the past quite often. If that is true, then it follows that changes in the past will also affect our present, which in turn affects our future, so action is occurring across all spectrums of time on a constant basis. It is only our limited perspective that makes it seem that events are sequential, with a precise beginning, middle, and ending like the story books we used to read as children. While there is a certain comfort to viewing life in such a way, that particular comfort blanket just doesn't work for me anymore.

In regards to highly charged events such as my rape experience, I think aftershocks ripple outward (or better yet inward) affecting all aspects of our being, although each aspect will react to events in their own way.

Going back to that Friday night get-together at Jane's, the Sumari stated that the bread had been stolen from the seagulls. When we take from others what we don't have a right to take, the bread is indeed stolen from the seagulls. In the case of my rape this certainly applies, and while ultimately we must forgive others for what others have taken from us, more importantly, we must forgive ourselves.

15

Tiny Bubbles

*If a bubbling spring, on reaching the surface of the earth said,
"Shall I burst up joyfully into the air or shall I watch my course? I
must watch myself and keep guard on myself, for who knows what
water is." Then you would all go thirsty and the poor stream would
not bubble up as merrily as it does. And I am looking at you and
using you only as an example, because I know what I say applies to
you, but it also applies to one extent or another to each of you.*

When Seth said "I am looking at you" in the above comment, the
"you" he was referring to was me, and his words rang all too true.

As an aside, I just want to note that Seth had an uncanny abil-
ity to point things out to people without them feeling put down
or criticized. Instead, you intuitively sensed that Seth was simply
trying to bring to your attention certain issues that you needed to
look at. And this was certainly the case here, as bubbling up merrily
was not a normal part of my routine. While for the most part I had
rejected Marcel's statement that I was "in the grips of a demoniacal
thing," I still kept a very tight net around myself.

I lived in fear of my own energy, afraid of what might happen if

I really let myself go. I was like a star afraid of its own light. Thank goodness stars don't feel that way or we'd all be walking around in darkness.

As I've said before, energy does not like to be bottled up and will always seek a way out. That is its nature. When it is allowed to flow freely there is no problem. It is only when we hold our energy in check for too long that it has a tendency to explode, or implode, and give rise to the type of unfortunate consequences we were hoping to prevent. And that is the sad irony here: that any threat to our safety and well-being doesn't come about from *the release* of our energy, but from *our attempts to stifle it*. But as long as I continued to hold the belief that allowing my energy to flow freely represented a threat to my being, then bubbling up merrily was not going to be an option.

Seth's words about the "bubbling spring" helped me begin to realize the extent to which I had imprisoned my energy, holding it hostage, and posting a guard to ensure that the "prisoner" did not escape. How often I wished I could relieve that guard from his duty. He has been faithfully standing at his post for what feels like centuries. He rarely goes on vacation, is up at the crack of dawn, and doesn't sleep until I sleep. In some ways I admire his single-minded dedication. He stands straight and tall with his gun at his side, and takes pride in his never-ending vigil. And when the inner stream of spontaneity threatens to bubble up and escape its bonds, all he will allow are tiny bubbles, releasing just enough pressure so the whole damn structure doesn't blow up.

Yet tiny bubbles just weren't enough anymore. I wanted to "bubble up merrily." But for that to happen I had to start trusting the natural flow of my energy, which meant trusting the natural flow of my mind.

I often felt as if I was suffering from some peculiar form of mental gridlock. While you won't find the term "mental gridlock" in any medical dictionary, being quite familiar with its symptoms, I can offer you the following definition: **mental gridlock** is a condition of the mind where your thoughts become so jammed up they are unable to move. You feel like your consciousness is stuck on a one-lane highway behind a painfully slow-moving vehicle, which at times is not moving at all. In some cases of mental gridlock you are able to peek inside the car ahead of you, the one holding up the works, and you inevitably discover that the person sitting behind the wheel bears a striking resemblance to yourself. In the most advanced cases, when the flow of interior traffic remains at a standstill over a prolonged period of time, you can experience a breakdown of the entire mental mechanism.

In regards to mental gridlock, or any disease or set of symptoms, be they mental or physical, I believe a common element in all forms of illness is a strong resistance on the part of the personality to deal with certain issues on a conscious level. I believe that symptoms reflect attempts by the personality to bring particular issues to the forefront of the conscious mind so as to be able to resolve them. The unpleasant nature of the symptom makes it difficult, if not impossible, for the personality to continue to ignore the problem, in a sense "forcing" the personality to then confront inner conflicts that thus far it has not been willing to deal with directly.

I also think that the personality adopts various symptoms in a misguided effort to protect itself, believing that if the personality were to relinquish the symptoms, it would be opening the door to even greater pain and suffering than that which it is currently experiencing. As long as the personality believes the symptom is keeping it safe from an even greater harm, then the current symptom will not only be accepted as a necessary condition, but also the personality will cling to the symptom despite its debilitating effect. Unwilling to risk the greater pain and suffering we believe will follow should we relinquish the symptom, we make a tradeoff, strike an inner bargain, accepting the present symptom with the understanding that by doing so we are protecting ourselves from greater suffering down the road. The fact that the current suffering as well as the projected future suffering are in truth unnecessary is often not an easy point for the personality to fully comprehend. I believe the personality employs the same "logic" as described above regarding any unpleasant condition or circumstance that exists as part of our lives on a chronic basis.

In regards to my belief that that my energy could not be trusted, that to allow it free rein was to court disaster, I adopted "mental gridlock" as a means of protection. I had great difficulty discarding this belief for the same reasons described above that one has difficulty discarding a physical symptom they have held onto for many years. Time and again I tried to change this belief by using my powers of reasoning and the force of my intellect. But irrational fears can be quite impervious to rational thought, no matter how well-framed one's arguments might be. There is a point one simply has to throw caution to the wind and take the plunge.

There are waves of mental energy within us that rise and fall like the tides. If we allow ourselves to ride those waves we will discover that place within us where the stream of life bubbles up merrily. As children we played in that stream every day.

One night in class I was talking about wanting to reconnect with that sense of magic I felt as a child. In response to my comment Seth said the following to me: *We will see that you do, so that you will not have to look back for the rest of your life with envy toward the ecstasies of your youth.* The universe was speaking to me, and its voice wasn't riding on tiny bubbles but on waves of ancient energy, reaching the shores of my consciousness with unmistakable force and power. While I couldn't say I understood all the meanings within the words that were being spoken, one thing I did understand: I was no longer walking down dead-end roads; and when those waves of energy were done speaking and I'd get up to leave class and head back to New York City, I would be leaving with a lot more than just a hatful of rain.

16

The Mark of Zorro

When I was about nine years old I used to watch this television series called *The Mark of Zorro*, which was based upon a silent motion picture released in 1920. Zorro was a swashbuckling swordsman who left his special mark, a "Z," carved upon the face of each evildoer he defeated. Although I once took fencing lessons and enjoyed them tremendously, the desire to carve a Z (or any other letter) upon the face of another never rose up within me. But what did rise up within me was a desire to leave my own special mark upon the world. During class one evening I spoke of this desire, and Seth came through with the following comment:

Now, your being is important! The fact that you are, my friend, impresses the universe, and that impression is never lost. Your being, as it is, is important, and whatever you do, it is not trivial.

I didn't doubt the wisdom of Seth's words, but "important" was not how I felt about myself. A meaningless blip on some cosmic radar screen was closer to the way I viewed my existence. In my early teens, in response to such feelings, I engaged in various forms of exaggerated behavior. While such behavior did at times result in my standing out from the crowd, it did not eliminate my feelings of insignificance. As I got older, continuing to act out in such a fashion only served to make me look foolish. I then looked for confirmation of my worth in the eyes of lovers; in praise from my parents; in approval from my peers; but none of these approaches seemed to work either.

So I tried still another tack. I set goals for myself that if achieved would surely (so I thought) bring about that sense of self-approval I so desperately sought. But I set the bar so high, demanding so much of myself, that falling short was a foregone conclusion. The resulting "failures" then led to more rounds of self-recrimination, reinforcing the original belief that my being was of little importance.

Over the years I knocked on a thousand different doors in search of this elusive creature called self-worth, but no one ever seemed to be at home. I finally realized that the sense of affirmation I was seeking was not going to be found behind *any* outer door but resided within the inner doors of my being. When I started to open those inner doors, I discovered, among other things, an operating system whose main function was to tend to the mechanics of reality creation. While far more sophisticated than any operating system one would find in even the most advanced computers, they shared something in common. No matter how efficient the operating system might be, the results it could achieve were dependent upon the nature of the programs that had been installed. And the more I continued to look at the programs running inside of me, the more I realized a lot more was needed than just a few minor updates.

While the operating system worked just fine, and the scripts I had written were being faithfully executed, the nature of those scripts brought forth results that left much to be desired. I needed to create an entirely new set of scripts based on codes that addressed reality in an entirely new way. For example, when faced with various choices, I needed to start making decisions in accordance with *my* beliefs, rather than allowing myself to be bullied by the opinions of others or blown off course by the prevailing winds of custom or tradition. I had to start approving of the characteristics that were unique to my being rather than trying to twist myself into some mold or model that society deemed desirable or proper. And I needed to realize that I was not some meaningless blip flashing across some cosmic radar screen in some faraway galaxy, but that my being was important, and nothing that I or anyone else ever did was meaningless or trivial.

Your Being Is Important should be written across the blackboards of every school in every country, with gold stars given out to all students caught writing those words on the side of a bathroom wall.

Your Being Is Important should be painted in big bright letters on billboards alongside every highway and flashed from neon signs above the streets of every major city.

Your Being Is Important should be whispered in the ears of every child from the moment they are born until the day they die. Let those words ring out from the rooftops of every shack, shanty, outhouse, whorehouse, courthouse, and jailhouse across the globe until their meaning becomes indelibly written upon the mass consciousness of the world.

There are those who walk this earth alone. They live their entire lives never knowing the comfort of warm arms wrapped around them on a cold wintry night. There are those who draw breath, but for all intents and purposes have fallen off the face of this earth. They live and die in small rooms, and like shadows that pass in the night, their own passing garners little attention. There are those who have forgotten how to love, with empty windows in their heart, where none look in and none look out. Yet every one of those people is important. Every person you will ever meet or gaze upon, whether they sit on top of a throne or wake up each morning mired in their own filth, is a living mosaic that forms an integral part of the fabric of this universe. Every thought they think is like a star illuminating the night sky, creating roads of light for all of us to walk upon.

EVERY SINGLE PERSON ON THIS EARTH is not only important but of equal importance. There can be no caste system when it comes to evaluating the worth of another. Don't create one for yourself.

Your being IS important . . . and so is mine. Let's celebrate. My place or yours?

17

Go With My Blessing

One of the topics that was coming up in class with increasing frequency was the subject of beliefs. Part of the reason for this may have been the fact that Jane was in the middle of writing *The Nature of Personal Reality*, a book dictated by Seth in which beliefs were being discussed extensively. According to Seth, beliefs are the building blocks we use to create our reality, and thus their significance could not be overstated.

I began to wonder: if our beliefs were lined up in the proper way, were there any limits as to what we could create? Change our beliefs about food and voila... we could eat gobs of chocolate cake and never gain a pound. Change our beliefs about money... and there's our picture in the newspaper as the latest lottery winner. Come to think of it, I wouldn't mind being a bit taller. Change a few beliefs ... and up I go. As I thought about all of this during class one night I asked Seth the following question:

RICH: If I believe that I can go up to a lonely mountain that nobody inhabits, and that in ten years' time a beautiful woman with purple hair and purple eyes is going to walk by and fall in love with me; if I believe it strongly enough, is it going to happen?

SETH: *If you believed it strongly enough, and if you did not find it easier to accept a woman with a different color hair, and if there were not a reason why you could not simply accept a normal love on a normal street corner, and if you are willing to offset all the other connections and believed it deeply enough, then go with my blessing!*

So there it was. With the right beliefs in place there seemed to be no limits as to what we could create. I could go to that mountain with full confidence that after ten years' time a beautiful woman with purple hair and purple eyes would miraculously appear and we would spend the rest of our lives together in unending bliss.

There would of course be a few details to work out first, beginning with which particular mountain this event was going to take place upon. In my question to Seth I spoke of a "lonely" mountain. To be honest I don't really know what the hell I meant by a "lonely" mountain or how I'd distinguish a lonely mountain from one that wasn't, but my beliefs would sort all that out so I didn't have to worry about it. I'd automatically be directed to the right mountain.

Another potential concern was the fact that I had never done any mountain climbing before, in addition to the fact that I had an acute fear of heights. But a quick change in beliefs and in no time at all I'd be rappelling with the best of them.

Yet while entertaining such thoughts, another part of me was asking myself: could it really be that easy? Perhaps the question itself betrayed the fact that deep down, or maybe not so deep down, I didn't really believe this could happen.

As I continued to work with my beliefs I often did feel as if there was a mountain I had to climb—a mountain of beliefs—and that I would never get to the top. Yet I don't think there is a top in those terms. As Seth once said, he was not trying to get us to disbelieve in beliefs, just to discard those that led to limitation and embrace those that led to expansion.

In regards to the purple-hair woman scenario, I want to share with you an event that occurred some years later. I had fallen into a trance far more dangerous than any trance a medium might encounter; in other words, I had fallen in love. I'll call her Stephanie to protect the innocent, although no one in this drama was totally innocent. One night we were getting ready to go to a Halloween party. Stephanie was in the bathroom with the door closed for what seemed like an eternity as she was putting on her costume. I had no idea what she was going to be wearing. When the bathroom door finally opened, it was as if a door from another dimension opened at the same time. And from out that other door this woman started walking toward me with the most intense looking PURPLE HAIR I had ever seen. I just stood there transfixed. There she was, my purple-haired lady come to life!

Although the purple hair was simply a wig she had bought earlier that day, imagination and reality coalesced in a way that transcended the usual lines we draw between fact and fiction. And with Stephanie not knowing anything about the exchange that had taken place between me and Seth that evening in class, further questions arise as to how much information our consciousness is privy to despite the seeming barriers presented by time and space.

Another point worth mentioning is the way I interpreted this event. At the time, I took it to be a clear sign from the universe that Stephanie and I were destined to be together for the rest of our lives. Signs and symbols, however, should not always be taken at face value, something I learned a few months later when Stephanie and I went our separate ways. I was beginning to think that having a good relationship was just not in the cards for me, yet I reminded myself that I was the one dealing the cards. So I went back to the drawing board for what seemed like the zillionth time and shuffled the deck once again.

As long as I've touched upon my love life, let me also share with you a dialogue that took place between Seth and me at another class. I was speaking about my belief that in order for me to have a successful relationship with a woman, she would have to subscribe to Seth's ideas. Here is what Seth had to say on the subject:

Do not insist, as you have been, that a woman understand my words—only that she understand the messages that spring from her own soul. If a woman understands the messages of her own soul, what is there that you could require? Understand the messages from your own soul.

Understanding the messages from my own soul sounded like an awfully tall order. I would have much preferred to have Seth or some kind of cosmic messenger call me up one day and say, "Rich, this is the Big Guy from the sky. I have deciphered the messages from your soul and will be happy to drop them off whenever it would be convenient for me to stop by."

> RICH: "Hey, Big Guy, that's great news! I've been waiting a really long time to hear from you. I'll be home all afternoon and all evening."
>
> BIG GUY: "Super."
>
> RICH: "Let me give you my address."
>
> BIG GUY: "Uh oh, I think we have a problem."
>
> RICH: "Problem?"
>
> BIG GUY: "In my enthusiasm to help I momentarily forgot to mention that we don't deal with where or when anymore. They became so annoying over time that we decided one day, or was it one night, to just drop them. So having your address won't really work."
>
> RICH: "But you must have some way of getting in touch with people."
>
> BIG GUY: "Of course we do. We try to get in touch with them all the time. We talk to them in dreams, we send them impulses, and occasionally we even send out some dude like Seth; you know the guy who ..."
>
> RICH: "YES, I KNOW."
>
> BIG GUY: "My, my. Feeling a bit cranky today?"
>
> RICH: "Look, could we please get back to the messages from my soul?"
>
> BIG GUY: "Oh, I didn't know we left them."

RICH: *"Earlier* (yes I know, you don't deal in time anymore) you said *RIGHT NOW,* at this exact moment, that you had deciphered the messages from my soul. Why don't you just take what you have written down and email them to me? Email isn't really the same as a physical address so that should allow us to get around the problem quite nicely."

BIG GUY: "I'm really not trying to be difficult, but I never said anything about *written* messages."

RICH: "Okay, just give me a few seconds. I'll grab a pen and some paper, and you tell me what I need to know, and I'll write it down. How does that sound?"

BIG GUY: "I appreciate your persistence but the problem with that solution is that I'm quickly running out of minutes on my cell phone. There simply isn't going to be enough time during this call to tell you all the things I'd like to say."

RICH: "Wait a second. You just told me a minute ago that time doesn't exist for you anymore."

BIG GUY: "What I said is true; we don't deal in time or space anymore, but YOU do, and we have to take that into consideration. You still believe that your life is defined by minutes and hours and miscellaneous points on a compass, and as long as you believe such things we have to respect your beliefs."

RICH: "Do me a favor, just this once—don't respect my beliefs. Just forget my beliefs and do whatever you need to do."

BIG GUY: "But that would be quite rude on my part and I wasn't brought up that way."

RICH: "Be rude, please. I'm giving you full permission to completely disregard any beliefs I hold that might interfere with this exchange of information. Forget all the rules of cosmic etiquette you were brought up with, just this once. I promise not to tell a soul. It will be our little secret."

BIG GUY: "But I don't believe in secrets anymore. Listen, I'm going to run out of minutes very shortly, but before we get cut off I'll make you a deal. Meet me in the dream state tonight and we'll talk. Have your agent call my agent and we'll sort this whole thing out."

RICH: "But I don't have an agent."

BIG GUY: "You might be happier about that one day than you imagine. But that's neither here nor there."

RICH: "Wait! Please don't go. Did I mention that I'm contemplating climbing this mountain where this beautiful woman lives who has purple hair and purple eyes? I'd be more than happy to have you come along. We can talk then. What do you say ... Hello? Hello ... Damn."

18

A Wig of a Different Color

The following excerpt is from the book *Conversations With Seth* by Susan M. Watkins:

She was a pale ghost of a girl, sitting passively on the floor, a bright green paisley scarf tied over her dark red hair; her face so flat, pasty white that I had to force myself not to stare at her in disbelief. She was a visitor in class and although it was nearly 10 PM, she hadn't said a word, although I'd noticed her talking at length to Jane during break.

I too found it difficult to take my eyes off her. When she first sat down and introduced herself she mentioned something about having Hodgkin's disease but I wasn't sure what that was. At some point in the evening Jane started to sing in Sumari, directing the song to this girl. As Jane was singing I kept staring at this girl's face, and for some reason an image of Joan of Arc came to mind. She was tied to a cross and had rope burns on her wrists. Her body was all bloody and bruised from being dragged across a dirt road. All her hair had been cut off, and her execution was only minutes away. A crowd had gathered in front of her, and they were staring at her bald head. I felt like I was peeking along with the crowd as I too was staring at Joan of Arc's bald head, but her face kept changing into the face of the girl with the Hodgkin's disease sitting across from me. The song ended; Jane put her glasses back on, and what happened next seemed to occur outside of time.

During the song, Jane/Sumari had been making motions in a kind of pantomime, pointing to the scarf on top of the girl's head. One of the students who was sitting next to this girl suddenly started to mimic the movements the Sumari had been making. He playfully reached over and pulled up on the girl's scarf, and in doing so, the scarf unexpectedly came off. BUT WHAT ALSO CAME OFF WAS THIS BRIGHT RED WIG THE GIRL HAD BEEN WEARING—EXPOSING HER TOTALLY BALD HEAD FOR ALL TO SEE. My consciousness just went reeling. I was momentarily stunned and literally confused. It was as if Joan of Arc had jumped across time zones and was now sitting in front of me. As in my purple-hair lady scenario, the line between fact and fiction had once again blurred. The girl went on to explain that the loss of her hair was due to the treatments she was receiving for her Hodgkin's disease.

Regaining my mental composure, a number of thoughts began to run through my mind. While I didn't think this girl was a reincarnation of Joan of Arc, similarities did exist. Both she and Joan of Arc were waiting to die with a certain kind of resignation that held neither resentment nor fear. There was also a certain kind of "innocence" they both possessed, a naïveté about the world, although I don't mean that in a pejorative sense.

I also started thinking about the conclusions that are drawn when someone has an experience that by its nature doesn't fit into the parameters of reality that society considers normal or sane. I'm speaking here of the conclusions drawn by the person having the experience. In the case of Joan of Arc, she asserted that she heard voices and had visions from God, charging her with a mission to recover her homeland from English domination. Claiming divine guidance, she testified she was visited by Saint Michael, Saint

Catherine, and Saint Margaret, also instructing her to drive out the English and bring the Dauphin to Reims for his coronation. I don't doubt for a moment that she experienced such visions and heard such voices, but her interpretation of those experiences is a different story. Jane Roberts, like Joan of Arc, also heard voices but never interpreted them as coming from God or some saint or even from some kind of "spirit guide" as that term is often used. Had she done so, the Seth material would have gone in an entirely different direction and would be lacking the depth and richness of thought that are evident throughout the entire body of work.

Drawing from Jane's own reflections on the subject, I think that when we hear voices or see visions, the psyche is personifying certain information or concepts, acting them out in such a way that the personality can grasp their meaning. Dreams are a perfect example of such personification, where symbols and dream events are used to dramatize various ideas; but when we interpret them literally, we can run into trouble. How different Joan of Arc's life might have been had she not jumped to a literal interpretation of the psychic events she experienced, as opposed to trying to find the symbolic meaning within them.

Now why the psyche speaks to us in such a fashion I do not know. It would certainly seem a lot more convenient if the inner self communicated to us using simple and direct language, which then *could* be taken literally. But perhaps in trying to ferret out the meaning behind the symbols and the dramas the psyche weaves, we lead ourselves to deeper understandings than if we had just received a literal message, which by its nature is one-dimensional in scope.

Many of us may never experience the kind of inner voices and visions that came to Joan of Arc, yet within each of us there are voices that speak and images that appear. Our interpretation of such phenomena may not be a matter of life and death as it was with Joan of Arc, yet nevertheless our take can greatly influence the directions our lives go in.

As I was writing this chapter there were moments when I had the distinct feeling that Marguerite de Valois was looking over my shoulder. Whether she was literally looking over my shoulder or in some way tuning in to what I was writing about I don't know. But as a young girl Marguerite would have heard many stories about Joan of Arc, stories which would have made a strong impression upon her. And on various occasions, like Joan of Arc, Marguerite took up arms and led soldiers into battle. I wonder if during such times, images of Joan of Arc danced in the background of Marguerite's mind.

I then saw this picture of a beautiful field filled with row upon row of vibrant wildflowers. In the center of the field three young girls held hands and danced in circles until they fell down laughing. They then picked themselves up and started all over again. Something about the phrase "starting all over again" seemed important, but my mind needed a rest. I just didn't want to think anymore, at least not tonight. Tomorrow I could start all over again.

19

The Voice of a Small Flower

There is a place within me where all movement stops. The leaves on the trees are absolutely still. The birds stare out in silence. All the streets are empty and all the shops are closed. No one lives here, except death.

I stumbled inside this place one evening during class, and although I did not speak of it, Seth looked at me and said the following:

> *Existence need not be torturous or unpleasant or painful. The voice of a small flower can send you into frenzies of being if you but listen.*

I heard his words but they did little to soothe my pain. Perhaps the voice of a small flower could send me into frenzies of being, but no flower has ever bloomed here. This is a place where I rage against God, but like the birds he stares out in silence. Sometimes I think this place will one day devour me, its invisible tentacles of hopelessness wrapping themselves around me so tight I will never be able to escape.

You can cry out in agony if you want.

Part of me wanted to do just that, but my pride prevented me from engaging in such a public display.

The voice of a small flower can send you into frenzies of being if you but listen.

Was that it? Was that the best Seth could offer me? At the least I wanted Seth to be an apologist for God, to explain how God could allow his creatures to suffer so deeply, yet no apology was being offered. When you live in a home where you feel you are not loved, you can always move out. But if you live in a universe that you feel doesn't care about you, where do you move to?

There are times I feel this dark place starting to tug at the corners of my consciousness, starting to reel me in. Yet there is a part of me that is also drawn to this place, despite knowing the pain that awaits upon my arrival. Part of me believes this is the place where all the secrets of the universe are kept, locked in some ancient vault, and the key to that vault will magically appear if I am willing to suffer enough (although when enough is enough is a question I don't have an answer to).

The road to Elmira was fueled in part by such feelings of despair. When I first started attending Jane's classes I hoped that Jane or Seth might one day be able to rid me of such feelings, but I came to realize that however well-intentioned Jane, Seth, or anyone might be, certain things we can only do for ourselves. This applied equally to Jane's relationship with Seth.

How wonderful it would have been to walk into class one night and see Jane dancing across the room, her body moving with the agility and grace of a professional ballet dancer, the result of Seth having removed all of her physical symptoms the night before. But as I said, there are limits as to what others can do for us, whether those others are in the flesh or outside of it.

If another could ride roughshod over our own beliefs, even if the result was a desirable one, then free will would be compromised, and without free will the whole concept of creating one's reality would lose all meaning.

As dark as the places might be that I fall into at times, and as trying as Jane's life became because of the physical difficulties that plagued her, I'd rather believe (as I know Jane did) that we are not victims of forces beyond our control. I know this can be an extremely difficult proposition to accept at times, especially when body or mind is racked with pain, but the alternative, that we can be at the mercy of something outside of ourselves (or inside of ourselves) is a proposition I am just not willing to accept.

20

Idiot Behavior

It was November of 1972 and once again we gathered in Jane's living room. On the world stage the Vietnam War was finally winding down. Within a few months the Paris Peace Accords would be signed by the U.S., North Vietnam, South Vietnam and the Viet Cong, effectively ending our participation in that war.

But a few years earlier the Vietnam War was in full swing, and military service was compulsory. This meant that if you were summoned by your local draft board to undergo a pre-induction examination to determine your fitness for military duty, you were legally bound to appear. Jeff, one of the regular students in class, read an essay one night recalling the events that transpired when he was summoned to show up for his pre-induction exam in 1968. Here is the essay Jeff read that evening:

> I saw little justification for the U.S. involvement in Southeast Asia on any grounds—ethical, economic, practical, theoretical, or otherwise. I rejected President Eisenhower's Domino Theory (an ill-defined term). Due to these reasons I

was not interested in doing my duty and serving my country in the Armed Forces. I also was not morally outraged enough to split to Canada or go to jail in protest.

In my last term at college, I was called for a pre-induction physical. This was it—the big moment I'd dreaded for so long. I had to determine a plan of action. I thought of opting for a medical deferment since I'd had a double hernia and a pinched nerve in my back, but I knew I was in good health and that method wouldn't work. Then I decided I would have to play freaked out. I had never acted before and I knew I would have to be convincing. It was my strong belief that I was going to get out of the draft without having to leave the country or go to jail.

I was called down at the same time as was Willie, a friend of mine. I stayed up all night and at five in the morning I dressed. I was unshaven. I put on sunglasses and a pink shirt and my flamingo-pink overalls. I wore no shoes or socks and a torn coat. I applied to my clothing and my person generous helpings of the following: scotch, mud, ketchup, vinegar, rubbing alcohol, urine and various other unusual cosmetics. I took the train, and the other passengers took one look or sniff in my direction and departed for the other end of the car. The one item that had the most distinct odor was a skin-disease cream called Leucoderm. I wanted to buy out the company and patent the product as a guaranteed draft repellent. I got some weird stares from Willie's parents when I got to his house. "Your friend's here, and he's wearing his pajamas and doesn't have any shoes," they said. When we got to the draft board waiting room, Willie said to pay no attention when your name is called, but go up to the desk for our papers after everybody else. We got to a room full of desks, and I sat at three different ones. I took the pencils from all of the desks around so the others had no pencils, whereas I had nine of them. I filled out the medical history form with checks and crosses in all the negative *and* all the affirmative columns. I also scribbled on the page and wrote lefty so I couldn't see how they could make any sense out of it. I checked off such items as homosexual tendencies, bedwetting, recurrent hallucinations, drug abuse, etc. Then we were to take the forms to a room where we were to strip down to our underpants (which I conveniently hadn't worn) and we were given a little cellophane bag to carry our valuables in.

I walked into the room, and as everyone else hung up their clothes and got in line, I stood there staring at the ceiling. After a while, someone came over and asked me what I was doing and I handed him the papers with the cellophane bag on top and stared at him. He told me to take my clothes off and I just stared at him in a petrified way and shook my head, no. They took me to a medical doctor who tried to persuade me to see the psychiatrist. I protested that I was deathly afraid of them. Finally I relented. The psychiatrist had long hair and a bushy mustache so l thought that he might be hip to me, but I stared at the floor and didn't look at him once and spoke in an almost inaudible voice. He looked at what I'd checked off: homosexual tendencies. "Have you ever had sex with a male at any time?" he asked. I said, "No, I want to, but I'm afraid." He asked, "Have you ever had hallucinations?" I said "I've seen frogs—and colors." "Do you take drugs?" "Sometimes." "Are you on drugs now?" "No." He was taken aback by that. He had difficulty believing that this was my normal behavior! Had I ever seen a psychiatrist? "No, I'm afraid they want to hurt me." Finally he gave me my papers after filling out a report which I read while walking through the halls: "Withdrawn, incoherent, wearing dark glasses, describes vivid hallucinations."

I received a 4-F: not qualified for any military duty, period. I related these incidents to illustrate in a personal way how one can have beliefs that prove themselves successful in practical physical terms. Incidentally, I feel patriotic about this because I felt any military career would turn out (for me) along these lines for real.

As you might imagine, Jeff's narrative elicited a variety of reactions, in some cases leading to some very heated debates. Some folks thought Jeff's behavior was utterly self-degrading, while others applauded him for following a moral imperative which they felt was fully justified. Here is Seth's take that evening on Jeff's behavior:

> *To do what he did does indeed appear crazy. Idiot behavior in the world that you know. But it is very sane behavior. If sanity is to lead your sons to death, then I would rather be insane any day!*

Another comment by Seth sparked a further round of lively discussions:

> *There is no way to insure peace but for every man, EVERY man, to lay down his arms.*

Rereading Seth's statement about every man laying down his arms, I began to imagine soldiers from every country banding together in a conspiracy to create a worldwide divestment of weapons. Under cover of the Internet, a program code-named *WMD*, standing for "Worldwide Military Disarmament," would be encrypted in seemingly innocuous emails and sent to all members of the armed forces in every country. Other emails would follow, which when decrypted would disclose detailed instructions on how to proceed, eventually specifying the exact date and time when this "offensive" was to be launched. I then envisioned some savvy reporter breaking the story and the panic that would no doubt ensue.

Governments that barely spoke to each other would suddenly find themselves in close cooperation, as top-level officials, military advisors, and weapons contractors from every continent would huddle together united by one common objective: to stop WMD in its tracks. Strange as it may sound, they would perceive such a universal laying down of arms not as a desirable event but as a threat to world peace. "How will we then be able to protect ourselves?" they would ask—unable to grasp the idea that there would no longer be anything to protect themselves from!

I know how divorced from reality all this sounds, but what is reality? Events begin within the mind and within the imagination. As long as we imagine that violence can act as an agent to bring about peace, then young men and women will continue to spill each other's blood as they have done for centuries. What is there to lose by imagining an army of young people from all corners of the globe joining together to rock the world with peace?

And if you're wondering how I fared during the Vietnam War era, I'll tell you.

Right around the time that Jeff received a notice to report for a pre-induction physical, I too received a notice to report. In truth, I really wasn't fit for military duty. Soldiers are trained to obey orders, and obeying orders has never been one of my strong points. More importantly, I did not consider the people of Vietnam as my enemy. I did not view them as a threat to either myself, my family, or to the United States of America. I had no desire to do harm to any of them.

So before arriving at my local draft board I employed similar techniques to those that Jeff had adopted. I covered myself with mud, didn't shave or shower for days, wore torn and tattered clothes, and applied all over my body copious amounts of the same skin-disease cream Jeff had used. As a finishing touch, the night before I was to appear I had a friend take out whatever condiments were sitting in his refrigerator and pour them all over me. My physical appearance combined with my wandering around the draft board halls like some lost soul with a severe case of amnesia was enough to result in my disqualification from military service.

I don't believe that violent confrontation, whether between individuals or between countries can ever lead to true peace. If peace is to be achieved, we must look to where wars originate, and that place is within the mind. Wars originate from the belief that we don't live in a safe universe; from feelings of powerlessness that tell us change can only come about from the outside; and from believing that by allying ourselves with some cause "greater" than ourselves we will find meaning and value to our lives. If Jeff's behavior was that of an idiot, I say IDIOTS OF THE WORLD UNITE! Let us dare to lay down our weapons and dance naked across the battlefields of the world. Now that's a *YouTube* video I would love to see!

21

GET OUT!

I had spent the night at a friend's apartment in Manhattan, and when morning came I stepped out on the terrace of her twentieth-floor high-rise, looking down upon the steady stream of traffic below me. The scene was a perfect metaphor of my life. I was trying to keep a safe distance between myself and all that was happening around me. I was determined to remain a neutral observer as opposed to becoming an active participant. The problem with positioning myself in such a way was that it led to an increasing sense of isolation, and at times I felt myself sinking into a loneliness that threatened to engulf me.

On the way to class that afternoon I thought of asking Seth for help but recalled his words one evening when he told me I had a tendency to rely too much upon him and not enough upon myself. So I was a bit surprised when after *not* asking for Seth's help, he came through and made the following comment to me:

> *I have a word for you tonight, when you did not ask for my advice. Get out! Go into the world! Seek your own sustenance. A*

nine-to-five job is not going to destroy you; how fragile you must think that you are!

I thought of my father and how he would trudge to work each morning, returning home at night too exhausted to do much more than eat his dinner, watch some television, and go to bed. I was terrified of falling into that same pattern.

Jane then turned to me and said the following: "Sometimes you have to grow older before you grow younger." Upon hearing those words an army of toy wooden soldiers began to amass along the borders of my psyche. With muskets held high at their sides they were determined to stand firm against the advance of the adult self, whose footsteps were growing louder with each passing day.

When you work with your beliefs, you will find that you have inhibited yourself and your natural curiosity about the world, out of fear that you are inferior and you are not ready.

For someone who hadn't asked for help I was sure getting the treatment tonight.

As to Seth's comment about my feeling inferior, I remember such feelings arising when I was about nine or ten years old, although I can't point to a specific event or series of events as the cause. But one thing was clear—my psychological house had been painted over with a new color, a color one might have aptly labeled "Deep Inferiority." My entire world became permeated with this new motif.

When I walked into a room it was as if I were holding a large sign in front of me with the word "INFERIOR" written upon it. In my interactions with others I often felt as if a giant spotlight was upon me, ready to expose my slightest misstep for all to see.

I then thought of something Seth had said to me during a personal visit with Jane and Rob. Although there was no Seth class scheduled for that day, a friend and I found ourselves with the impulse to drive to Elmira to see Jane. We knew that Jane and Rob tended to be very protective of their privacy, but with Jane speaking recently about the importance of following one's impulses, we decided to take her words to heart. We felt confident that when we knocked on Jane's door without any prior notice, she would let us in without any hesitation—and that is exactly what happened.

During our visit I spoke of how I wanted to feel "part of a meaningful universe." Unexpectedly, off came Jane's glasses and Seth came through with the following words:

> *You are not so much part of a meaningful universe, as the universe in part. That is the next step for you to joyfully follow.*

The more I thought about that statement the more I felt that within it was an answer, or at least the beginning of an answer, to some of the issues I had recently been struggling with. The distinction of being "part of" a meaningful universe as opposed to being "the universe in part" may seem to be a subtle point, but I think its significance is crucial in establishing a new view of the universe and a new view of ourselves. If each of us was the universe in part, then the universe or God wouldn't be something *outside* of us that we were then part of, nor would it be *inside* of us.

Inside and *outside* imply the existence of something separate, something apart from us; yet if we are "the universe in part," no such separation could exist. God and the universe would in effect be each one of us, a compilation so to speak comprised of endless individualities all coming together to form a totality that, while transcending the unique nature of each of its components, could not exist without them. And each individuality, be it of a person or a blade of grass, would be held in tender regard, never to be swallowed up as part of some merging with or return to God, for there never would have been a time we were separated. How could we ever be separate from that which is us? It would then be equally valid to say God needed us as much as we needed God, for without us God could not exist.

Relating these ideas to my concerns about being inferior, if we think of the cosmos as a multidimensional jigsaw puzzle and each of us as pieces of that puzzle, then every "piece," regardless of its size or shape or color, would be essential to the creation of the overall picture. From such a standpoint, comparisons between any of the "pieces" in terms of superior or inferior would be meaningless. Feelings of inferiority would therefore have no basis upon which to exist.

Seth once said, "Nothing exists in isolation," and I was beginning to understand that that included me as well. Rather than standing alone and watching that steady stream of traffic from the terrace of a twentieth-floor high-rise, I needed to get in the elevator, take it down to the main floor, and step out into the world. But to do so with confidence I would need to repaint my psychic house once again, replacing "Deep Inferiority" with a new color; and while my brushstrokes might not be executed with the precision of a Rembrandt, they would be my own—a unique addition to a magnificent canvas called physical reality.

And rumor has it that if you really pay attention, every now and then you might even see All That Is with brush in hand. I hear his technique can be a bit unorthodox at times, but hey, we can't all be Rembrandts.

22

Sleigh Bells Ring

Less than a block away from Jane's house, icy winds raced across the Chemung River, but inside all was cozy and warm. The room was bathed in a soft glow emanating from the multicolored lights that hung from the Christmas tree standing near Jane's rocker. I always liked the spirit of giving and goodwill that traditionally accompanied the Christmas season, but the religious ideas upon which many of those traditions were based were another story.

To begin with, the idea that Christ was born to atone for the sins of humanity was in my opinion a story spun from man's imagination, containing major distortions regarding the true nature of reality. Similarly, the idea that the rebirth of my soul was dependent upon pledging my allegiance to some deity outside of myself just didn't sit comfortably within my psyche. And the very thought of having to bow down before another, whether it was God, his son, his daughter, or his haberdasher, made every nerve in my body stand up and protest.

Seth often told us *we* are the gods. If we are the gods then there would never be a reason to kneel down before any presence, whether carved in stone, shimmering from stained glass windows, or nailed to a makeshift cross.

SETH: *Now, I prefer Pan piping his magic flutes over the countryside and drinking wine to a Christ born to be crucified.*

I say "amen" to Pan merrily piping his magic flutes across the countryside, yet in accordance with ideas presented in the Old Testament, ideas which have become fixtures in the mass psyche for the past 2,000 years, our time here on earth was meant to be a somber affair, with the soul being tested through various trials and tribulations. A joyful romp through the countryside was the last thing the writers of the Old Testament seemed to have in mind when describing earthly existence.

The deal seems to be as follows: for a short time at the end of each year the elves are busy in their workshop making all kinds of wonderful gifts which will bring joy and smiles to the faces of countless millions. For the rest of the year, God is busy in a different kind of workshop, thinking up all kinds of calamities he can foist upon mankind. And being creative, God would vary the nature of the afflictions he would visit upon the human race. For example, while the Black Plague or swarms of locusts might work well for a certain time period, they would at some point fall out of fashion, so God would replace them with other misery-causing scourges just as horrendous but better suited for the times. Next, God would have to decide who to afflict and who to spare. In light of the fact that we are told we are all sinners, that part of the process has me totally baffled. But moving right along, after putting the screws to a number of his "children," God would then spend a good deal of his time observing how the recipients of such misfortune would bear their burdens. Complaining too loudly or questions like "why me" were definitely frowned upon, as God sought reassurance that no matter how deeply one suffered, and no matter how long, God was still loved.

Sounds like a rather sadistic deity to me, with a voyeurism

bordering on the pathological, not to mention an insecurity complex requiring years of therapy. I have a feeling that whoever it was that introduced this particular concept into Judeo-Christian thought definitely woke up on the wrong side of the bed that morning.

Another example of someone waking up on the wrong side of the bed is the idea found in various religious writings that the more we suffer here on earth, the greater our rewards will be in the after-life. So when God was not busy devising new and improved plagues and pestilences to shower upon the earth, he'd be going through this vast cosmic logbook, locating the names of all those who had recently died. Using a special program Microsoft designed especially for God, he'd tally up all the suffering that each of the recently departed had endured during their time here on earth, and based on the results, the program would automatically generate a seating chart indicating where each of the deceased would be spending eternity listening to the harps play and the angels sing. The choicest seats of course would be the ones right by God's side, but these were generally reserved for martyrs as well as those few souls who for reasons unknown to this day were forced to watch reruns of *Harry and The Hendersons* for days on end with the volume turned way up.

Personally, I don't want to spend eternity sitting by God's side. For one thing, I get restless when I sit too long; my legs begin to twitch. And as far as the harp goes, while I happen to think the harp is a fantastic instrument, I'd miss the variety of sounds which have become part of mankind's musical heritage. Needless to say (although I'll say it) this notion that God has an interest in compensating us for our travails here on earth is a doctrine I do not subscribe to.

As the class continued, Seth spoke about the meaning of Christmas, and after the first break, the room lights were extinguished and we were directed to observe the lighted Christmas tree and see what thoughts or images came to mind. While doing this my consciousness began to drift, and a number of images came to mind. I saw dancers in a church, their white taffeta gowns moving in perfect unison to an unseen choir, reminding me of an experience I had while visiting the Mission in San Juan Capistrano.

I saw beautifully carved silver goblets filled with sweet wine being raised into the air, as prayers were being recited in a language I was not familiar with.

I then saw myself walking up a steep hillside along with hundreds of other people, each of us carrying a small cross fashioned from branches of white birch. When we reached the top of the hill all the crosses were placed one on top of the other and the entire pile was set on fire as the flames reached high into the sky.

SETH: *I think that when Santa Claus laughs, that is better than blood coming out of the heart, and pictures of the crucifixion.*

Depictions of Christ such as those described above have been revered by millions of people for centuries. Yet even the most cherished of iconic images can lose their luster when the beliefs that have given them their power begin to fade. We are not bound by historic events, be they fact or fiction. What we choose to focus on NOW is what matters, for what we focus on NOW reaches out to all realities, whether we think of them as past, present or future.

There was a Seth quote that Jane and Rob taped up to their bathroom wall which stated the following: ("You get what you concentrate upon.) There is no other main rule." I would rather concentrate on pictures of children laughing and singing beneath a brightly-lit Christmas tree than gaze upon portraits of Christ nailed to a cross with the blood flowing freely from his side.

I'd like to say at this time (hmm, sounding a bit like a politician here, that can't be good) but I do want to say that I know I can appear harsh at times in my criticism of traditional religious ideas. I also know that for millions of people these same ideas have great meaning and serve to comfort them during times of crisis.

While I do not apologize for any of my viewpoints, I do recall how Jane once cautioned us not to confuse the essence of another human being with the beliefs they may hold. What exists inside all of us transcends any set of beliefs and cannot be contained within the pages of any book, regardless of who is doing the dictating.

As my first year of attending Jane's classes was drawing to a close,

I had witnessed the death of many ideas, yet also witnessed the birth of many new ones. I had closed many doors, sometimes with great reluctance, but new doors always opened.

As I passed by Camp Lakota on my way back home that night I could sense my younger self quietly sleeping. When he awoke the next morning he may have wondered why he dreamed of icy winds and Christmas trees in the middle of summer—a summer filled with baseball, swimming in the lake, and toasting marshmallows around a midnight campfire. But his questions quickly disappeared as he began to think of those freshly baked rolls that awaited him each morning in the camp's dining room. Like presents from some invisible Santa Claus, a wonderful breakfast magically appeared each morning, and he never asked himself why or whether he deserved such bounty. He wasn't ready to start walking the path of self-sacrifice and self-denial. He was too busy drinking in the joys of each day. I kissed him gently on the forehead, and as I continued the ride back to New York City I wondered how long this journey to Elmira was going to last. I didn't have an answer to that question, but I knew I was at the beginning of something important, and I was determined to see it through.

23

The Train To Uncertainty

If physical reality is just a figment of our imagination, then perhaps imagination in its own way is as real as physical reality. With that in mind I find myself standing on the platform of a railway station. The stationmaster makes the following announcement: "Leaving from track number one is the Death and Taxes Express. Leaving from track number two is The Train to Uncertainty, making all local stops."

I can't say I was fond of either choice, but this was the only station in town and these were the only two trains one could take. Taxes were something I always had difficulty with so I decided to take The Train to Uncertainty.

"Final call for The Train to Uncertainty. And then again it may not be the final call. But if you are certain you want to board The Train to Uncertainty then you may be on the wrong train, but you still have time to catch the Death and Taxes Express."

I step inside The Train to Uncertainty and take a seat. As the conductor comes by to collect my ticket I realize I haven't bought one yet. I tell him I need to purchase a ticket and he tells me I already have one. The conversation goes something like this:

RICH: "I don't recall having purchased a ticket. When did that occur?"

CONDUCTOR: "It happened the moment you entered physical reality. All possibilities and probabilities were immediately set in motion upon your birth. Add to that the fact that new possibilities and probabilities are being born even as we speak, and you'll realize you already have a ticket to The Train to Uncertainty."

RICH: "Can you at least tell me what stops this train will be making? Surely there must be some kind of schedule in place."

CONDUCTOR: "Surely there is NOT, although you can get off wherever you wish, and spend as little or as much time at each stop as you desire."

RICH: "But how can I plan anything in advance when I don't know with any kind of certainty where this train is going?"

CONDUCTOR: "Sorry, old boy, I'm only paid to make sure the train keeps moving; the rest is up to you."

RICH: "How about this: if I tell you what stops I'm planning to make will you at least tell me what will happen at each stop?"

CONDUCTOR: "I couldn't possibly do that."

RICH: "Why not? Does that violate some kind of Conductor's Code as to what you can or cannot do?"

CONDUCTOR: "I can't tell you because I don't know. There is no way to determine exactly what will happen at any of the stops you may decide to make until you make them. Why do you think we call it The Train to Uncertainty? As I've said, my job..."

RICH: "Yes, you told me—your job is only to make sure that the train keeps moving. I have an idea—as we approach each station just nod your head in one direction or another so I'll know if it's wise for me to get off at a particular station. After all, you've taken this train before, so why not help a fellow passenger out when you can?"

CONDUCTOR: "Why would you think I've taken this train before? I never made such a claim. Remember what I said about new possibilities and probabilities being born all the time."

RICH: "If you can't tell me what will happen at each stop, could you at least tell me what's waiting for me when I reach the end of the line?"

CONDUCTOR: "Since I haven't been to the end of the line, and I'm pretty sure there is no end of the line, it's rather difficult for me to answer your question. Also, while I know it appears to be a line, between you and me it really isn't."

RICH: "I'm trying to get some clarification here but your words are just adding to the confusion I already feel."

CONDUCTOR: "Adding to your confusion is truly not my intent, but the line you speak of is more like a circle. And because the circle's radius is constantly changing, you can never really pinpoint exactly where you are because the moment you say "I am here," here is no longer here."

RICH: "I'm starting to get a headache."

CONDUCTOR: "Perhaps you should take an Excedrin. Then again, Tylenol might work just as well. It's like Ajax and Comet. Some say Ajax works better, others vote for Comet. I myself like to mix baking soda with just a dash of lemon juice. You'd be amazed how well that works. We even use it in the train sometimes to clean the seats. It leaves such a lovely scent."

RICH: "This is all quite fascinating, but you were talking about circles and how the radius keeps changing and I'm trying to understand but it isn't easy."

CONDUCTOR: "Think of a wheel and the spokes that are attached to it as railroad tracks going out in all possible directions toward a town called Infinity. (By the way, I was there last summer for a brief time and highly recommend it.) But getting back to your questions, you need to realize that whatever track you find yourself on at any given time will always be changing to reflect the changes that are occurring within yourself. And with change being the one constant you can depend upon, the only certainty that exists is the uncertainty that change brings along with it as part of its itinerary."

RICH: "I'm not a violent person but you're starting to get on my nerves in the extreme. Cutting through all your fancy words, the bottom line seems to be that no matter what I do, uncertainty will surround every stop I make, and if that is the case, then how can I ever trust the train that I'm on, the stops I may make, or even the tracks the train is traveling on?"

(Scene now fades and I find myself in Jane's living room. Seth comes through and makes the following comments to me, which he actually did one evening in class.)

The only way, with your attitude, you could trust existence was to live a life that you remembered completely in which you knew every event—the beginning, the middle and the end—and then, on the second time around, you would die of boredom! What do you want —an examination with the answers already given you ahead, or a game in which you already know before you even begin the game, whether you will win or lose?

YES, that is exactly what I wanted. I wanted to get off The Train to UNCERTAINTY and buy a ticket for The Train to CERTAINTY. The problem was that I was reluctantly coming to the conclusion that a Train to CERTAINTY simply did not exist. So a new question began to form in my mind: how do we make peace with the idea that whatever we do and whatever decisions we make, an uncertainty factor will always be there, like a faithful dog that never strays too far from our side?

Thinking of Seth's comment to me about wanting all the answers beforehand, I began to think that maybe life is supposed to have an uncertainty factor. Maybe all the mysteries that surround us were actually planted there by ourselves, and then pretending over time to forget where we hid them, we actually do forget. Then one day in the middle of this crazy cosmic game of hide and seek we decide to go looking for those answers, and in the looking we travel roads and stop at destinations that we otherwise never would have visited.

I was starting to get a headache again but it wasn't the kind of headache that Excedrin or Tylenol was going to take away. Like the Energizer Bunny commercials of the 1980s, instead of batteries it was my mind that kept going and going and going until I said ENOUGH, time out, I need a break.

The train I'm on at the moment has stopped at 458 West Water Street in Elmira, New York. How long it will be stopping there I'm not sure, so I'm going to walk over to the dining car to have lunch, and you are welcome to join me. I'll pay, but you leave the tip.

To be continued.

Acknowledgments

CHRISTOPHER STONE for his endless encouragement and excellent advice.

SUE WILLIAMS for her generous donation of time and energy in reviewing this manuscript.

MARY DILLMAN for her labor of love in working with the Jane Roberts Papers at Yale University. Her website can be accessed at sethapplied.com.

JASON ROGAN for his support on many levels.

EMMY VAN SWAIIJ for always believing in me.

Printed in the USA
CPSIA information can be obtained
at www.ICGtesting.com
LVHW092135290324
775868LV00003B/562

9 780983 577607